W9-BKR-047

Best Practices for Teaching

WRITING

Other Corwin Press Books by Randi Stone

Best Practices for Teaching Mathematics: What Award-Winning Classroom Teachers Do, 2007

Best Practices for Teaching Science: What Award-Winning Classroom Teachers Do, 2007

Best Classroom Management Practices for Reaching All Learners: What Award-Winning Classroom Teachers Do, 2005

Best Teaching Practices for Reaching All Learners: What Award-Winning Classroom Teachers Do, 2004

What?! Another New Mandate? What Award-Winning Teachers Do When School Rules Change, 2002

Best Practices for High School Classrooms: What Award-Winning Secondary Teachers Do, 2001

Best Classroom Practices: What Award-Winning Elementary Teachers Do, 1999

New Ways to Teach Using Cable Television: A Step-by-Step Guide, 1997

Best Practices for Teaching

WRITING

What Award-Winning Classroom Teachers Do

RANDI STONE

LIBRARY
FRANKLIN PIERCE COLLEGE
RINDGE, NH 03461

CORWIN PRESS
A SAGE Publications Company
Thousand Oaks, CA 91320

Copyright © 2007 by Corwin Press, Inc.

All rights reserved. When forms and sample documents are included, their use is authorized only by educators, local school sites, and/or noncommercial or nonprofit entities that have purchased the book. Except for that usage, no part of this book may be reproduced or utilized in any form or by any means, electronic or mechanical, including photocopying, recording, or by any information storage and retrieval system, without permission in writing from the publisher.

For information:

Corwin Press
A Sage Publications Company
2455 Teller Road
Thousand Oaks, California 91320
www.corwinpress.com

Sage Publications India Pvt. Ltd.
B 1/I 1 Mohan Cooperative Industrial Area
Mathura Road, New Delhi 110 044
India

Sage Publications Ltd.
1 Oliver's Yard
55 City Road
London EC1Y 1SP
United Kingdom

Sage Publications Asia-Pacific Pte. Ltd.
33 Pekin Street #02-01
Far East Square
Singapore 048763

Printed in the United States of America

Library of Congress Cataloging-in-Publication Data
Best practices for teaching writing: What award-winning classroom teachers do / [edited by] Randi Stone.
    p. cm.
Includes bibliographical references and index.
ISBN 978-1-4129-2460-3 (cloth) — ISBN 978-1-4129-2461-0 (pbk.)
    1. English language—Composition and exercises—Study and teaching (Elementary)
2. English language—Composition and exercises—Study and teaching (Secondary)
3. Effective teaching. I. Stone, Randi. II. Title.

LB1576.B4857 2007
428.0071—dc22

                                             2006034234

This book is printed on acid-free paper.

07 08 09 10 11   10 9 8 7 6 5 4 3 2 1

Acquisitions Editor:	Faye Zucker
Editorial Assistant:	Gem Rabanera
Production Editor:	Melanie Birdsall
Typesetter:	C&M Digitals (P) Ltd.
Copy Editor:	Bill Bowers
Proofreader:	Cheryl Rivard
Indexer:	Michael Ferreira
Cover Designer:	Scott Van Atta

Contents

Preface

In the pages that follow, award-winning teachers generously share their best teaching practices with us. I hope you enjoy reading about their classrooms and trying out their teaching techniques as much as I have.

Acknowledgments

Thank you to a wonderful group of teachers for sharing your stories with us.

About the Author

 **Randi Stone** is a graduate of Clark University, Boston University, and Salem State College. She completed her doctorate in education at the University of Massachusetts, Lowell. She is the author of nine books with Corwin Press, including her latest in a series: *Best Practices for Teaching Writing: What Award-Winning Classroom Teachers Do*, *Best Practices for Teaching Mathematics: What Award-Winning Classroom Teachers Do*, and *Best Practices for Teaching Science: What Award-Winning Classroom Teachers Do*. She lives with her teenage daughter, Blair, in Keene, New Hampshire.

About the Contributors

Sharon Andrews, Fifth-Grade Teacher
Challenge Center at Mark Twain Elementary
315 West 27th Street
Sioux Falls, South Dakota 57108
School Telephone Number: (605) 367-4560
E-mail: andresha@sf.k12.sd.us

Number of Years Teaching: 13
Award: Presidential Award for Excellence in Mathematics and Science Teaching, 2003

Christine Chaney, Third-Grade Teacher
East Side Charter School
3000 North Claymont Street
Wilmington, Delaware 19802
School Telephone Number: (302) 762-5834
E-mail: cchaney@escs.k12.de.us

Number of Years Teaching: 17
Awards: New Castle County, Delaware Spirit Award, 2004
MBNA Best Practices in Education, 2002
Education Unsung Heroes Award, 2002

James W. D'Acosta, Social Studies Teacher
Fairfield Warde High School
755 Melville Avenue
Fairfield, Connecticut 06825
School Telephone Number: (203) 255-8449
E-mail: jdacosta@fairfield.k12.ct.us

Number of Years Teaching: 17
Awards: Celebration of Excellence Awards by the Connecticut
State Department of Education in Economics and in
American History, 2001
Harvard Teachers Prize by the Harvard Club of Southern
Connecticut for Inspiring "Intellectual Curiosity and
the Quest for Excellence in Students," 2000

Elizabeth F. Day, Sixth-Grade Teacher
Mechanicville Middle School
25 Kniskern Avenue
Mechanicville, New York 12118
School Telephone Number: (518) 664-6303
E-mail: eday@mechanicville.org

Number of Years Teaching: 29
Awards: New York State Teacher of the Year, 2005
Who's Who Among America's Teachers, 2005
WNYT, Channel 13, Educator of the Week Award, 2003

Stacy Gardner Dibble, Fifth-Grade Teacher, Reading Coordinator
Prairie Elementary
1700 1st Avenue S.W.
Worthington, Minnesota 56187
School Telephone Number: (507) 727-1250
E-mail: stacy.dibble@ISD518.net

Number of Years Teaching: 17
Award: ING-UnSung Hero Award Winner, 2005

Dara Feldman, Kindergarten Teacher
Garrett Park Elementary School
4810 Oxford Street

Garrett Park, Maryland 20896
School Telephone Number: (301) 929-2170
E-mail: dara_feldman@mac.com

Number of Years Teaching: 21
Awards: Disney Outstanding Elementary Teacher, 2005
National Board Certification in Early Childhood, 2004
Computerworld Smithsonian Award in Education and
Academia, Christa McAuliffe Fellow, 2000

Rosemary Fryer, English Teacher
Heritage High School
7825 NE 130 Avenue
Vancouver, Washington 98685
School Telephone Number: (360) 604-3400
E-mail: rfryer@egreen.wednet.edu

Number of Years Teaching: 27
Awards: National Teacher Hall of Fame Finalist, 2005
USA Today All-USA Teacher Team, 2003
Washington State Teacher of the Year Program, 2003
Regional Teacher of the Year, 2003

Vicki Goldsmith, English Teacher
Roosevelt High
4419 Center Street
Des Moines, Iowa 50312
School Telephone Number: (515) 242-7272
E-mail: Vicki.goldsmith@dmps.k12.ia.us

Number of Years Teaching: 41
Awards: Bowling Green State University Accomplished
Graduate Award, 2006
National Teacher of the Year Finalist, 2005
Iowa Teacher of the Year, 2005

James Darrell Harris, Special Education Teacher, Department Chair
Atkins Middle School
5401 Avenue U
Lubbock, Texas 79412

School Telephone Number: (806) 766-1527
E-mail: jdharris@nts-online.net

Number of Years Teaching: 38
Awards: Honorary Doctor's Degree
Outstanding Alumni—College of Education,
Texas Tech University
Teaching Excellence Award, Horace Mann Foundation

Carla Hurchalla, Coordinator of Instructional Technology
Wicomico County Board of Education
900 Mt. Hermon Road
Salisbury, Maryland 21804
School Telephone Number: (410) 677-4420
E-mail: churchal@wcboe.org

Awards: National Board Certified Teacher
Christa McAuliffe Fellow

Brenda Lynch, Spanish Teacher
Madison High School
800 N.E. 9th
Madison, South Dakota 57042
School Telephone Number: (605) 256-7706
E-mail: Brenda.lynch@k12.sd.us

Number of Years Teaching: 15
Award: American Association of Teachers of Spanish and
Portuguese South Dakota Teacher of the Year, 2000

Ganna Maymind, First-Grade Teacher
Asher Holmes Elementary School
48 Menzel Lane
Morganville, New Jersey 07751
School Telephone Number: (732) 972-2080
E-mail: ganna15@hotmail.com

Number of Years Teaching: 5
Award: Donald Graves Award for Excellence in the Teaching
of Writing, National Council of Teachers of
English, 2005

Diana W. McDougal, Art Educator
  East High School
  2800 East Pershing Blvd.
  Cheyenne, Wyoming 82001
  School Telephone Number: (307) 771-2663
  E-mail: Diana_mcdougal@bresnan.net or
  mcdougald@laramie1.k12.wy.us

  Number of Years Teaching: 25
  Awards: National Art Education Association, Board of
           Directors, Pacific Region Vice President-Elect, 2004
         National Professional Teaching Standards Board
           Certification, Early Adolescence Through
           Young Adulthood/Art, 2000
         Marion Quinn Dix National Professional Art
           Leadership Award, National Art Education
           Association, 2000

Mary Merrill, Kindergarten Teacher
  Crescent Park Elementary
  19 Crescent Lane
  Bethel, Maine 04217
  School Telephone Number: (207) 824-2839
  E-mail: merrillm@sad44.org

  Number of Years Teaching: 16
  Awards: Who's Who Among America's Teachers, 2006
         Maine State Wal-Mart Teacher of the Year, 2005
         Disney Teacher of the Year Nominee, 2005

Susan Okeson, Principal of Chugiak Elementary School
  Chugiak Elementary School
  19932 Old Glenn Highway
  Chugiak, Alaska 99567
  School Telephone Number: (907) 742-3400
  E-mail: Okeson_Susan@asdk12.org

  Number of Years Teaching: 16
  Award: Anchorage Chamber of Commerce Top 40 Under
         40 Award, 2005

Micheline P. Plaskett, Library Media Specialist
John M. Gandy Elementary School
201 Archie Canon Drive
Ashland, Virginia 23005
School Telephone Number: (804) 365-4652
E-mail: mplaskett@hcps.us

Number of Years Teaching: 15
Award: The Education Connection Educator Award for
            Excellence in Integrating Cable Television and
            Learning, 1996

Beverly R. Plein, Technology Facilitator
Benjamin Franklin Middle School
1315 Taft Road
Teaneck, New Jersey 07666
School Telephone Number: (201) 833-5089
E-mail: bplein@bellatlantic.net

Number of Years Teaching: 20
Award: Milken Family Foundation National Educator Award,
            2003

Carly Pumphrey, First-Grade Teacher
Marlowe Elementary School
9580 Williamsport Pike
Falling Waters, West Virginia 25419
School Telephone Number: (304) 274-2291
E-mail: cpumphrey@adelphia.net

Number of Years Teaching: 8
Awards: ING Grant Recipient, 2005
            Pocalla Springs Teacher of the Year, 2000

Peter W. Riffle, L. S. Teacher
Wilson High School
2601 Grandview Boulevard
W. Lawn, Pennsylvania 19669
School Telephone Number: (610) 670-0185
E-mail: rifpet@mail.wilson.k12.pa.us

Number of Years Teaching: 38
Awards: VFW National Teacher of the Year, 2005
Pennsylvania VFW State Teacher of the Year, 2005
Disney American Teacher Award Special
Education Honoree, 2000

Pam Roller, Second-Grade Teacher
Galveston Elementary
401 South Maple Street
Galveston, Indiana 46932
School Telephone Number: (574) 699-6687
E-mail: rollerp@sesc.k12.in.us

Number of Years Teaching: 32
Awards: Japan Fulbright Memorial Fund Teacher Participant,
2005
Disney American Teacher Awards Honoree, 2003

Nancy Rushing, First-Grade Teacher
Mt. Pleasant Academy
605 Center Street
Mt. Pleasant, South Carolina 29464
School Telephone Number: (843) 849-2826
E-mail: nancywycoffr@yahoo.com

Number of Years Teaching: 39
Awards: Wal-Mart Teacher of the Year for South Carolina, 2005
Mt. Pleasant Academy Teacher of the Year, 2004

Barbara Sabin, Kindergarten Teacher
Crescent Park School
19 Crescent Lane
Bethel, Maine 04217
School Telephone Number: (207) 824-2839
E-mail: sabinb@sad44.org

Number of Years Teaching: 32
Awards: Bethel Chamber of Commerce Teaching Excellence
Award, 2005
Disney Teacher of the Year Nominee, 2006

Nikki Salvatico, First-Grade Teacher
General Wayne Elementary
20 Devon Road
Malvern, Pennsylvania 19355
School Telephone Number: (610) 647-6651
E-mail: nsalvatico@gvsd.org

Number of Years Teaching: 10
Awards: USA Today All-USA Teacher Team, 2005
Pennsylvania Teacher of the Year, 2005
Citadel Heart of Learning Award Nominee, 2005

Burt Saxon, High School Teacher
Hillhouse High School
480 Sherman Parkway
New Haven, Connecticut 06511
School Telephone Number: (203) 946-8484
E-mail: burtsaxon@aol.com

Number of Years Teaching: 35
Award: Connecticut Teacher of the Year, 2004–2005

Eric Stemle, High School English Teacher
Evanston High School
616 Lucille Circle
Evanston, Wyoming 82930
School Telephone Number: (307) 789-0757
E-mail: estemle@msn.com

Number of Years Teaching: 30
Award: Wyoming Teacher of the Year, 2003

C. Joyce Taylor, Sixth-Grade Teacher
Cook Elementary School
3517 Brooken Hill Drive
Fort Smith, Arkansas 72908
School Telephone Number: (479) 646-8880
E-mail: jjtaylor40@cox.net

Number of Years Teaching: 30
Awards: Wal-Mart Teacher of the Year for the State
                  of Arkansas, 2005
                  Phi Delta Kappa International, Western Arkansas
                  Chapter, Elementary Teacher of the Year, 2005

Linda K. Voelker, Language Arts Teacher
Indian Woods Middle School
9700 Woodson
Overland Park, Kansas 66207
School Telephone Number: (913) 993-0600
E-mail: lindavoelker@smsd.org

Number of Years Teaching: 36
Awards: Unsung Heroes Award (ING Program), 2005
                  Friend of Special Education (SMSD Gifted Program),
                  2005

To my precious daughter Blair and new beginnings

CHAPTER *1*

Anonymous Responses Enrich Learning

Burt Saxon

New Haven, Connecticut

S tudents are both eager and reluctant to discuss very personal matters with their classmates. For years, I have used an activity called "Anonymous Response" to encourage students to share personal experiences—often uncomfortable ones—with their peers.

The activity is a simple one. A topic comes up—most often in psychology class, but once in a while in U.S. history—which is likely to be difficult to discuss. The letters "AR" go next to the topic on the board, which lets my students know that they will be receiving a blank piece of paper during the class. A typical topic would be "My Thoughts About Death." "Teenage Sex," "Marijuana," and "Alcohol" also are appropriate topics. The students also have the option of writing "do not read" at the top of the paper. This gives me permission to read the paper to myself, but not permission to read the paper out loud.

I tend to read several papers out loud before pausing for discussion. But occasionally most of the papers will require a pause for discussion. Only once in the last 20 years did I ask students to identify themselves as the writers. I read several papers on the topic "My Thoughts About Teenage Depression" and then reread two.

Once I recommended that the writer see the school social worker. But after rereading the second paper, I insisted that the student either see me after class or make an appointment with the school social worker. I have been amazed at the quality of the writing I have received. Writing an anonymous response takes no more than five minutes, yet many of the responses have been polished essays.

Giving your students a chance to express themselves on personal matters without revealing their own identities makes perfect sense both educationally and psychologically. I strongly recommend this activity to both high school and middle school teachers.

CHAPTER 2

Historical Fiction Using Scenario Groups and Annotated Bibliographies

James W. D'Acosta

Fairfield, Connecticut

Challenges

- Getting students to invest themselves in the lives, circumstances, and decisions of our forebears.
- Demonstrating the value of historical documents.

Solutions

- Using historical fiction to get students emotionally involved with the past.
- Creating fun experiences with historical documents.

A scenario group is a group of students pretending to occupy the same historical time, place, and situation. Each student faces the situation from a different point of view. For example, the place may be Nottoway Plantation on the Mississippi north of New Orleans in Louisiana, and the group may consist of three juniors in an American history class studying slavery.

One student pretends to be a member of the master's family, another is a slave, and the third is a visitor from Connecticut. Each student writes two or more fictional letters or diary entries based on research materials that I provide in class: tourist brochures of Nottoway or access to books or Internet sites with images of the plantation, copies of newspapers from the period containing advertisements for runaway slaves and slave auctions, and slave narratives such as that of Frederick Douglass.

Students help each other gather historical facts, but they must remain in character in their individual writing assignments. Staying in character forces each member of the group to recognize the complexity of the historical situation: Slave masters were motivated by concern for the economic well-being of their families, peer pressure from their neighbors, safety, and habit when confronted with the question of continuing to use slave labor.

Slaves considered separation from their family and friends, not knowing where to go, how to get there, or what they'd do once they escaped, and the terrible consequences if captured. Visitors were restrained by manners, peer pressure, and severe legal penalties if they helped a slave escape. The Scenario Group Handout I give to students includes:

1. *Slave:* Pretend you are a slave on the plantation pictured on the brochure. Write about your life, the work you do, and about your hopes and dreams for the future.

2. *Owner:* Pretend you are a member of the family who owns the plantation and lives in the house pictured on the brochure. Write about your life, the work you do, and about your hopes and dreams for the future.

3. *Visitor From Connecticut:* Pretend you grew up in Connecticut. You are familiar with the Amistad Revolt. You are visiting the plantation pictured on the brochure, perhaps as a friend of the family, a cousin, or a hired professional such as a teacher. Describe what you see and give your opinion about slavery.

Consider the following events when deciding on dates for your letters or diary entries. The character from Connecticut must display knowledge of the Amistad Revolt and should therefore choose a date after 1838.

1793	Eli Whitney invents the cotton gin.
1801	Haitian Revolution begins under Toussaint L'Ouverture.
1822	Denmark Vesey's plans for a massive slave revolt in Charleston, South Carolina, are discovered and crushed.
1831	Nat Turner's bloody slave rebellion in Virginia.
1839–1842	Amistad Revolt, trials, and return to Africa.
1850	Harriet Tubman begins as a conductor on the Underground Railroad.
1852	Harriet Beecher Stowe's abolitionist novel, *Uncle Tom's Cabin,* is published and inflames public opinion.
1857	Dred Scott Supreme Court decision.
1860	Abraham Lincoln is elected president on a Republican platform promising no slavery in the territories.
1861–1865	Civil War

In class, I provide students with copies of the May 24, 1840, edition of *The Daily Picayune,* New Orleans's newspaper, brochures of plantations including Nottoway and Oak Alley in Louisiana and Monticello and Stratford Hall in Virginia, and a variety of slave narratives such as Frederick Douglass's. My handout to students includes a Research Notes Organizer, on which they note facts they may use in a letter or diary entry and enough information about the source to fulfill the required format in their annotated bibliography.

Assessment is ongoing and individual. I measure each student's learning by noting diligence in gathering information, the level of cooperation within each group, and the quality of each student's individual research and written work. A large part of what makes this assignment fun is the freedom afforded by historical fiction. The plot is up to the students. Writing about the motivation and mechanics of a desperate escape gets students emotionally involved in slavery.

The annotated bibliography requiring students to list a certain number of facts gathered from a minimum number of sources helps them focus on historical documents and sources. A fact for which a student can claim credit may be as simple as the presence of a second-floor balcony at Nottoway. The presence of the balcony is verified by photographs of the home.

In a diary entry, a student may have a character jump off this balcony. A slave bludgeoning an owner with a silver candlestick in the dining room, someone picking up a particular piece of furniture, or someone running down a hall in a certain direction to get outside—all these mention features of Nottoway and yield facts for the student's annotated bibliography.

CHAPTER 3

Five Circles, Five Paragraphs

Christine Chaney

Wilmington, Delaware

During the last decade, I have recognized an increasingly notice-able emphasis on empowering students to be able to enhance their academic achievements to become motivated lifelong learners. Along with this challenge, there has also been a strong desire to reduce the persistent achievement gap between students coming from more affluent middle- and upper-income families or backgrounds and low-income minority students.

With the Internet readily available in classrooms today, communi-cation connections between countries all across the globe are growing rapidly. These new trends make effective communication on the part of teachers, students, and eventually business or corporate employees even more important than ever before.

These growing trends caused me to recognize the pressing need to teach effective writing strategies early in a student's education to truly help close the achievement gap and enhance communications with others around the world.

For many years, I have taught what I consider to be one of the best methods of teaching writing. Positive evidence to back my judgment of a better method comes in the form of my third-grade students consistently performing well above the average statewide scores in the mandatory and annual Delaware State Testing Program (DSTP) over the past five years.

I am a third-grade teacher at East Side Charter School, located in the heart of a low-income neighborhood in the city of Wilmington, Delaware. Nearly 85 percent of our students qualify for free or reduced-cost meals under the federal guidelines for the National School Lunch Program.

Not long ago, the school's executive director and I had a heart-to-heart conversation regarding the need to increase our students' communication skills and ways to motivate them to want to learn better writing skills. We decided to implement a writing format that would not only enable our third-grade students to write a five-paragraph essay but to also have fun doing it. Hence, the five circles and five paragraphs writing formula was adopted as the basis for writing an essay.

With this formula in place, all students in the third grade, regardless of their actual reading and writing level, are taught to write five-paragraph essays. High expectations are set for each student, and they seem to learn well writing with this style. As the formula was introduced and lesson plans were created around this idea, I noticed more effective writing emerging from the children as they wrote their stories.

First, I demonstrated to the students how to plan an essay using a five-circle planning sheet that would be our focus to prepare for writing the essay. Using large chart paper, I drew five large circles and explained what each would be used for. The main purpose of each was for (1) introduction, (2) detail, (3) more detail, (4) even more detail; and, finally, (5) the story's conclusion.

For several writing sessions, the students watched and listened to me as I planned out my own essay before them. During my planning sessions, I explained what to write in each circle for the introduction, details, and conclusion. Each essay topic was based on something that was currently happening around us in school or in the classroom.

For example, when I started this process in December, we had just experienced the largest snowstorm of the season and school had been closed for two days while snow removal took place all around the city for the buses to get through.

On our first day back, we discussed what we had all done during the days off outside in the snow. We then wrote about the different things we could have done out in the snow. After several sessions of planning and interrogation, each student had several favorite ideas of how and what to write about, and they were able to fill the five circles of their own papers with their personal ideas and events, whether they had actually experienced them or simply desired to if they had thought about them.

Helpful Tips

- Introduce the writing format slowly and over a period of several joint writing sessions based on the actual needs of your average student.
- All writing prompts should relate to something the children have already been exposed to or to things they already know a lot about. Keep the subjects familiar.
- Introduce the concept to the parents. If parents understand how the concept works, they too will be able to help their children, even if they have never mastered the technique of positive communications themselves.
- Make as many positive comments about their writing as possible to maintain their desire for more. All students love to compete.
- Permit the students to read their essays to the class and to other groups. Invite parents to the classroom to hear their students' stories, and above all:
- Keep it fun!

CHAPTER 4

Reading and Writing Oasis Classroom

Linda K. Voelker

Overland Park, Kansas

While a warm glow from table lamps illuminates the faces of my students sprawled across the frames of overstuffed chairs or propped against luxurious pillows, several pairs of students across the room are in the conference lab either editing their writing or consulting about the books they have read.

In another section of the room, the soft blue lights of computer screens reflect onto the faces of students as they draft their stories. The first step to making this reading and writing oasis a reality for my community of readers and writers is a wide variety of books. I teach Advanced English 7, and I have focused on collecting books in multiples of 10 for three major reading areas: science fiction/fantasy, classics, and survivor novels.

Whether selecting a novel for the science fiction/fantasy reading group (*Eragon* by Christopher Paolini), a classic (*The Good Earth* by

Pearl S. Buck) for an annotated text, or a survivor book (*My Sister's Keeper* by Jodi Picoult) for an in-depth PowerPoint presentation, a wealth of books, readily accessible, will not only enrich students' knowledge base but also encourage students to use critical thinking skills.

A classroom generously stocked with a wide selection of books will encourage students to use their reading skills to seamlessly blend imagination, creativity, literary elements, figurative language, dialogue, and editing as they craft original pieces. "I love the bookcases in our room! I always know I can trust you to suggest a great book, a book I don't want to put down," said many students this year. The end result is students who develop a lifelong relationship with reading and writing.

When selecting books for this program, I suggest having 10 copies of at least 10 different novels for whatever genre or theme a teacher identifies through curriculum objectives or interest. A big factor in motivation is allowing students to make personal choices.

The second step in this vision of a reading and writing oasis classroom is to realize that middle school students are creatures of comfort. Their bones grow before their muscles, and they are always twisting and stretching at their desks, trying to get their muscles to match their bones. A few upholstered chairs and floor cushions scattered about will certainly address this need.

Access to computers is the last component of my integrated program. I will never forget the look on one girl's face when she sat down to use a laptop computer. When I stopped by to visit for a moment, she said, "I love to use the laptops. I feel so professional."

I see my students visiting other classes and schools to present book talks, student/teacher/parent book clubs forming, and speakers from our community visiting my classroom to expand on topics and issues highlighted in the books the students read. Then I am the facilitator, mentor, and, yes, teacher of a reading and writing oasis classroom.

CHAPTER 5

Teaching . . . Profession and Passion

Dara Feldman

Garrett Park, Maryland

T eaching is more than just my profession, it is my passion! I have an insatiable desire to increase my understanding of the art and science of teaching and am constantly researching and reflecting on ways to improve my practice. I recently achieved National Board Certification in Early Childhood. Working on my Boards was one of the most rewarding professional experiences I have ever undertaken because it gave me the opportunity to really focus on developmentally appropriate best practices and to strengthen my ideals of teaching.

I believe that all students can learn and that success does not look the same for each student. In order to help my children become successful in kindergarten, I let them know that I love them and believe in them. I teach them strategies they can use in school and in life. By focusing on students' interests, needs, strengths, learning styles, cultural backgrounds, and previous experiences, I nurture them to work to their full potential, and to care and cooperate with one another, thus helping lay the foundation for their lifelong learning.

I believe that my seamless integration of technology on a daily basis is something that makes my kindergarten classroom innovative and unique. Creating electronic books and movies with my students on a regular basis nurtures creativity, imagination, collaboration, communication, cooperation, and inspiration. For example, since 50 percent of my class is English Language Learners (ELL), many of my students were having difficulty learning positional words.

As a class, we brainstormed ways we could help our struggling classmates. My five-year-olds chose to make a video, using iMovie software and an Apple iBook computer. They storyboarded what it would look like, and then everyone took turns videotaping, starring in, and editing the movie.

We even made up a little jingle for our auditory learners and used special text features to expose the children to the spellings of each word. We posted the movie on our Web site so that we could watch it over and over again and so that other kindergartners could use it as well. I am happy to report that all my kindergartners now know all their positional words.

I know that I cannot meet the diverse needs of my students alone. I truly believe it takes a village to raise a child. I also believe, however, that in this day and age, it also takes a village to support families. With the ever-changing demands of twenty-first-century life, many of my students come from families of single parents who are working two jobs, families who don't speak English, families with financial struggles, as well as families who find it difficult to support their kindergarten children within the framework of our rigorous early childhood curriculum.

Now, more than ever, I feel it is vital to maintain regular, ongoing, open, two-way communication with my families, starting even before their child enters kindergarten. I want families to feel welcome, comfortable, and connected right from the start! So, during our spring kindergarten orientation for incoming kindergartners, I continuously play a PowerPoint slide show.

The slide show is an electronic book that my current kindergartners and I have created using the process of shared writing and including photos I have taken throughout the year. We also print copies in book form so the incoming kindergartners have a book about their new school to take home. Giving books to the children about their new school helps ease their anxiety and gives them an idea of the wonderful learning opportunities that lie ahead for them next year.

On the cover of our "We Love Kindergarten" book, we include my e-mail address so parents can e-mail me their individual questions and concerns. We also include the URL to our class Web site (homepage .mac.com/dara_feldman), which has a wealth of information, resources, and activities for kindergarten students, families, and other early childhood professionals.

As the late Helen Taylor said in 2000, "Technology is more than a tool and much more than a game. Technology is freedom. Without it our children will have a hard time in this world." I have witnessed firsthand how empowered early learners feel when using a developmentally appropriate digital content that scaffolds their learning and guides them to success.

Multimedia allow children to proceed as a function of their own interest, prior knowledge, and skills, thus controlling their own learning. As a facilitator of learning, I provide the appropriate tools and allow students to work with one another to develop their own understanding. It is especially empowering to children when they have created and are actually part of the multimedia.

They are extremely proud when their work is shared via our Web site so that their families and friends, both local and in other countries, can access it. To ensure that learning continues over the summer, I make copies of all the photos, movies, and electronic books we have created throughout the school year and give them to each student on the last day of school, either on a CD or VHS. Children and their families love to watch and reflect on how much they have grown and learned during kindergarten. E-mail helps us stay connected even after they have moved on!

Children also record themselves reading the books, which provides additional scaffolding for early emergent readers. For my ELL students whose native language is not English, other classmates and I create individual books and movies with and about our ELL students to help them learn vocabulary, concepts about print, and a variety of content-specific concepts and skills.

It is amazing how quickly they learn when they are part of the subject! It is wonderful to see how other students in my class are so excited when their classmates start speaking a little English. They feel as though they were directly responsible, and they were!

As the family outreach coordinator for my school, I have developed a variety of family involvement activities with regards to the arts, science, math, and literacy to strengthen the home-school connection and help parents help their children.

Parents and students participate in learning activities together, enjoy quality family time, and are important members of a community of learners. Working together on authentic and meaningful projects prepares students not only for high-stakes testing but also for successful lifelong learning.

I love to collaborate with others to engage students in learning. I do this in a variety of ways. As the kindergarten team leader, I facilitate weekly team meetings where we discuss students, their work, curriculum, family involvement, and other relevant issues. We share ideas, resources, and strategies. We compare work samples and observe one another's teaching and provide feedback.

We create electronic activities as a team, and then modify them to meet the individual needs of our students. As a member of the larger school system community, I often share presentations and resources I have created with teachers via our county's e-mail system.

They often modify my materials and share the changes they have made with others. Teachers from around the country visit my classroom to see how I integrate technology. I always learn something as a result of our debriefing sessions afterwards. It has been my experience that during collaboration, resources and strategies just keep improving!

In my role as president of the National Association for the Education of Young Children's (NAEYC) Technology Special Interest Forum, I cofounded the forum's listserv in 1997, and we have been having industry-changing discussions with more than 400 colleagues from all over the world ever since.

Creating the listserv allowed us to collaborate throughout the year, not just during the annual conference. As a result, we have created a truly collaborative Web site where early childhood educators lead discussions, share research and information, and demonstrate best practices regarding technology so it can be used to benefit children from birth through age eight.

We have worked closely with the leadership at NAEYC to help them use technology in meaningful ways with young children as well as for professional development purposes. As an Apple Distinguished Educator, I have been blessed with the mentorship of other outstanding technology using educators from around the world. Whenever I have a question or an idea to share, I send an e-mail and in minutes I get a response.

In addition, I am often consulted for information specific to technology and young children. I have gotten several requests from people around the world to use articles and presentations that I have created and posted on my Web site. I am currently working with a woman from Malaysia as part of her advisory committee for her master's degree program. I have never met her, not even spoken with her on the phone, but we have gotten extremely close electronically through e-mail. I hope she has learned as much from me as I have learned from her.

Because of my experience with young children and technology, I am often asked to be part of advisory boards and to collaborate with digital content providers to help make their programs better for young children. Some of the companies I have collaborated with include Edmark, Apple, Inspiration, and Apte.

I use technology to collaborate with families on a regular basis. I work hard writing grants and finding creative solutions so that all my families have a computer at home. Every day I send home an electronic newsletter and often get replies about individual students. I also send home weekly progress reports, which ask for family feedback. Our weekly homework has a place for feedback about the level of interest and difficulty for each assignment.

I often use technology to extend learning. In 2002, we had a severe winter with many feet of snow. School was closed for at least a week, so I sent an e-mail to families stating that due to the weather, we would be holding kindergarten online. Our plans were to write thank-you letters to our chaperones from the previous day's field trip.

As a springboard for writing, students could access the movie online that I had created about the field trip. The next activity students were to do was to go around their houses to measure things with various items such as pennies, crayons, and spoons. Next, because we were working on nursery rhymes in reading, they were to choose a nursery rhyme to memorize. I sent them a link to www.enchantedlearning.com, where they could access nursery rhymes. Their final assignment was to make snow sculptures. Not even snow could stop kindergarten that week!

Technology is such a powerful collaboration tool that it even allowed me to partner with the mother of one of my kindergarten students, who lived in Japan. Seo had not seen his mother for almost six months, so I took pictures of him engaged in school activities. He and I would collaborate to write e-mails to his mother about what he was doing in school.

When Seo moved back to Japan, my students and I e-mailed him on a regular basis, comparing what we were doing in the United States with what he was doing in Japan. We learned a lot about Japanese culture and how to write friendly electronic letters. Many of my students would e-mail Seo from their home computers, and still do. Collaborating with Seo was an incredibly moving learning experience for all of us.

During the past 20 years of my teaching career, I have had many experiences that have touched my heart and left an enduring impression on me. During the first month of my first year of teaching, I was teaching fourth grade at a Title I school. One morning, a child in my class came up to me in tears and told me that his mother had died. He then asked me if I would be his mother. I was fresh out of college and had never dealt with a situation of this nature.

I immediately ran to the counselor for guidance. She suggested that I read *The Ten Best Things About Barney* and do a lesson on death. I did what she suggested and then after school called his home to see what I could do to help. A woman answered the phone and I shared my condolences. She seemed taken aback, and to make a long story short, I was speaking with the child's mother. She had not passed away. My student had lied. At first, I was angry and confused but then realized that his lie was a cry for help. It was at that moment that I truly understood that my job had more to do with loving than learning. I had to work hard to help my children feel that they were loved and teach them how to learn to love themselves and others. That was the only way I was going to get through to these children, many of whose basic needs were barely being met.

Over the course of that year, I worked closely with this child. Because he exhibited a lot of mistaken behavior and needed a lot of reinforcement, I put him on a contract. He earned points each day toward special activities that we would do together, such as going to football games and having lunch. By the end of the year, he had made a lot of progress and was no longer telling lies to get his needs met. I continued to mentor him throughout his elementary school years and think about him to this day.

Two years ago, I had a student who reminded me a lot of that fourth grader. This kindergarten student never smiled, always said, "I can't," had very low self-esteem, and had no friends. Fortunately, I was taking a course called Studying the Skillful Teacher and learned about Attribution Retraining.

I worked extremely hard to help this kindergartner learn to believe in himself and taught him specific strategies that helped him learn that effective effort leads to achievement! As time went on, my student began to smile, make friends, take risks, and participate in activities. In March of that year, a new student joined our class who had an affect similar to the one this student once had. Both boys were in the same reading group.

About 10 years ago, a different chain of events left an enduring impression on me and caused me to make enormous changes in my teaching. My school got 25 Macintosh computers. At that time, I didn't even know how to turn one on, so I went to a three-hour training session. It was during that three hours that I saw the possibilities that technology possessed for my kindergartners.

CHAPTER 6

Connecting Students to the World That Lies Ahead

Beverly R. Plein

Teaneck, New Jersey

There was energy in the classroom that could be felt by everyone. Students were filled with excitement as they made last-minute adjustments at their computers. Some students worked alone, others together. Listening to the conversations in the classroom indicated that students were doing real work and understood the task at hand. They were motivated and eager to do their best.

As students got up to make their presentations, audience members immediately became quiet and were anxious to see and hear what their classmates had done. Even the most timid student felt a sense of trust and accomplishment, giving them the courage they needed to make their presentations.

Genuine applause and compliments were shared without teacher reminder. Thoughtful questions were asked and unexpected connections were made. It was obvious that the students were enjoying this month's book talk, which included the addition of a digital collage illustrating the elements of their book with their written book review.

This is not the way it always had been in this language arts classroom. At the beginning of the year, many of the students were unfocused and distracted, and some had discipline issues. A significant amount of time each day was spent talking about appropriate classroom behavior and the reasons for learning how to be a better writer.

The teacher tried a variety of instructional strategies, but the students did not seem interested in reading and writing. Some students were below grade level, so accommodations were made to match abilities and expectations. The teacher tried to provide differentiated instruction, but this was a time-consuming task that was difficult to manage and often unsuccessful. Students did not seem to connect what was going on in the classroom with what was important to them in their world.

As a technology facilitator, I help teachers use technology to connect what students want to learn with what they need to learn. Communication skills will be more important than ever if our students are to be successful citizens in the twenty-first century. Because the Internet will provide alternative ways for businesses to communicate, students will need to effectively articulate what they mean in a clear and concise manner using both written and verbal skills. Access to unlimited information will require individuals to evaluate information for accuracy as well as read for understanding. As teachers, we need to provide opportunities for students to work in collaborative settings while developing relevant, high-quality products.

Reading, writing, listening, and speaking skills can be enhanced with the integration of technology in the language arts curriculum. Begin by considering what skills you want your students to learn, why they need to learn each skill, and how the students will use the skill in the future. Think about creating an activity or scenario that will have a real-world application. Reading books will be more meaningful when students have a chance to "chat" about the book using a class blog or message board.

Do this as part of a class activity, and students will continue to write about the books even in the evenings and on weekends. Learning will happen outside the classroom because you have chosen to use a modality that students like to use and are comfortable with. Imagine students text messaging one another when they get to an exciting part of the book. It can and will happen when teachers make learning relevant to their students.

Consider telling students that a popular newspaper is considering creating a column for students to review books, and then have them write book reviews. Let them know that you will publish successful reviews online. Research shows that students will be motivated more and strive for a higher level of achievement if you publish their writing.

Digital storytelling is an effective way to engage students in the writing process. After discussing the elements of a good story, students decide on a topic and begin writing. Because the end product incorporates pictures, sounds, and music—all forms of media that the students enjoy using—they are motivated to write a story that is meaningful and engaging. The story follows the usual steps of the writing process, including draft writing, editing, and revision.

Students can use PowerPoint, a photograph slide show program, or video software to create the story using digital images, photographs, scanned artwork, and sound. Students develop their verbal skills when they record the narration of their stories. Posting the stories online will enable parents, grandparents, and students from around the world to hear your students' stories. Consider collaborating with a social studies or science teacher and have students create stories about heroes in history or the effects that a famous scientific discovery had on the world.

A digital camera can be a great asset to a classroom. It can be used to take pictures of important events as well as day-to-day occurrences. Consider taking pictures of your students during the first week of school, and then keep the files in an easily accessible place for use throughout the school year.

As an orientation lesson to computers, consider having students insert their photograph into Word and then create a "callout" bubble that includes a class rule that they think is important. Print out the student work and hang it up on a bulletin board. Students will feel greater ownership of the class rules because they wrote them, and parents will be impressed to see their children's work when they come for Back to School night.

Helpful Tip

■ If you are concerned about students plagiarizing from the Internet, have them submit their work electronically in addition to the paper format. Copy and paste the sentence that you believe was plagiarized into Google and it will return Web sites that have similar word combinations. Click on any suspicious sites to determine how much of the paper was plagiarized. This method is quick, easy, and cost-free.

CHAPTER 7

Writing Connections

Nancy Rushing

Mt. Pleasant, South Carolina

O ne would think that learning to begin to write would be simple. Students are able to talk and almost all can tell a story or relate an event with at least some accuracy. Then why is writing so difficult for some? Perhaps the underlying skills needed to be an effective writer have not been completely acquired.

To write easily and fluently, a student should develop a variety of prerequisite skills. These skills need to be carefully analyzed and then developed. Perhaps the child has difficulty seeing the connection between talking and writing and has difficulty thinking of ideas to write or how to organize ideas. The skill of expressing ideas on paper can be quite abstract for a child. As the child succeeds, confidence will be gained in the ability to write. Current standards rightly expect teachers to teach all students to write with certain proficiency. Examining the process of writing can help us do that.

There are many skills a child needs to acquire in order to write effectively. The child needs to listen to a variety of types of literature read aloud and should be involved in analysis and discussions of this literature on a regular basis. The child should be able to write legibly, not beautifully but legibly.

He or she needs to be able to spell simple words and also to be able to sound out more difficult words with enough accuracy that they can be read within the context of the passage. Consequently, instruction in spelling and phonics is vital. The child should be able to write a sentence with correct capitalization and punctuation fairly consistently.

Practice in composing a written sentence as well as writing dictated sentences helps to develop this skill. The skill of identifying the naming and telling parts of a sentence is also helpful. Practice in these skills should be ongoing, but I believe all these skills should be somewhat developed before formal instruction in *creative* writing begins.

Once a child is ready to begin formal instruction in creative writing, there are several steps that will help the child understand the task at hand. I always begin each new task by modeling the skill. One of the skills the child needs to develop is to write on the assigned topic. To help a child learn to write on a topic, I have them begin by writing a sentence using a given word.

The list of spelling words for the week is a good source for these words. I encourage the child to just write a simple sentence at this point, mostly using words he or she knows how to spell. (The dog is big.) Once this can be completed successfully, the assignment can be expanded.

Next I give the children a topic and ask them to write exactly two sentences about that topic. (Write about winning a race. Write exactly two sentences. Use these words when you write: run, first.) When the child can write two sentences in this manner, I expand the exercise to three words and three sentences.

This gives children practice in writing, consciously forming sentences, and writing on a topic, and it also challenges them to see how words can fit together. After the assignment is finished, I encourage them to illustrate their stories. This provides a connection between art and storytelling and the child's written word.

Helpful Tips

- Whiteboards and markers are wonderful tools when practicing spelling words or sentence writing skills. They are also useful when practicing handwriting. A letter or word can easily be erased or rewritten on these. If a letter is out of proportion, the simple dragging of a finger will make that part disappear and demonstrate the error to the child.

- I dictate sentences all year using sentences made with words from the spelling word lists. The dictation tasks may vary from one child to another. One child might write the whole sentence, another a single word, while another may write the first or last sound of one of the words.

- Another issue that needs to be addressed is the enjoyment of writing. Instilling confidence in a child needs to be carefully done. With reluctant writers, I take care to point out "great ideas" that they express aloud. I tell them I *can't wait* until they learn the skills they need to be able to write those ideas.

- I say that I can tell they are going to be great writers by the ideas I hear them talk about. When one believes that one *can do* something, one is more likely *to do* that thing. More attention needs (as in all things) to be given to those actions that the child has done correctly rather than things that have been done incorrectly.

- I try to point out *three* things I like, even if it's just the formation of a letter before I ask for *one* thing to be changed. For young children, especially, I ask for only one change at a time. I note skills needing work and provide practice for a skill at sometime other than writing time. I might, though, remind the child of the needed skill just before we write again.

CHAPTER 8

Verbs to Vocation

Using Spanish Verb Tenses to Create an Authentic Cover Letter

Brenda Lynch

Madison, South Dakota

*A*s a teacher in a small South Dakota town, I perpetually try to make the Spanish-speaking world meaningful to my students. I want them to understand that Spanish is not only a language in a book but also a culture with millions of people speaking this language. Students need to know that history, art, music, and practically every academic discipline can relate to Spanish.

I make my Spanish students three promises for their lifetimes, no matter where they will live:

1. They will have customers or clients who speak Spanish coming to their employers.

2. They will travel to places where they will meet Spanish speakers.

3. Either they or their children will have personal relationships with people who speak Spanish.

By the end of Spanish II, students have studied a range of grammar topics and verb tenses (present, preterit/imperfect, future, conditional, present/past perfect, present/past progressive, commands, and subjunctive). It is easy to get so caught up in "covering the material" that I decided to create an assignment to demonstrate how these tenses and grammar topics can work together to have a practical application in a business setting.

The first day we begin with a checklist of grammar topics to be included. To begin the letter, we brainstorm proper correspondence wording techniques (i.e., how to write the date, address people in a formal manner, and utilize power words for getting a job). The first paragraph is to be written with an introduction of themselves, a description of their personality, and why they are qualified for the position. The tenses of the verbs in this paragraph will review present, present progressive, and present perfect. They will also need to include an indirect or direct object with a verb.

The second day is the second and third paragraphs to review the two types of past tense in Spanish (preterit and imperfect). The second paragraph is about the onetime completed actions, which should use the preterit and past perfect verb tenses. This is likely to include graduating, honor/prizes/scholarships, travel, and unusual events that relate to a profession.

The third paragraph is written in the imperfect and past progressive tenses to demonstrate their previous jobs, lessons, and personal traits or experiences that have taken place over the course of time in the past.

The third writing day includes the fourth paragraph, which uses the future and conditional verb forms to tell an employer what you will do or could do for them. The final paragraph gives a suggestion using a subjunctive sentence and gives a command to call or grant an interview. They are then asked to exchange papers and peer-edit before typing the next day.

We use the computer lab to type the cover letters, and I ask all students to bold and underline each verb and grammar topic they are having graded from the original checklist. They are to print two copies of these cover letters: one to be graded and one to exchange with an assigned classmate. I use a differentiated learning technique to pair students of various levels for a homework assignment.

Basic-level students have to read the letter and create five questions they can ask the other person. Intermediate-level students are asked to create five questions to ask their partners, but the questions have to involve various verb tenses. The advanced-level students need to memorize five questions they can ask their partners. On the final day of the project, I have them interview one another at my desk while the other students are preparing their notes and study guide for their trimester exams.

I would eventually like to incorporate a handheld PDA component into this project, so students would be able to view other résumés and conduct mock interviews. It would also be encouraging if Spanish-speaking employees could review these letters to show how Spanish is used outside the classroom, possibly via e-mail.

Helpful Tips

- Distribute and read an actual cover letter written to an employer (I use my own, on file in the district office). This lends some authenticity to the assignment and helps the students understand how a cover letter can be organized.
- I want students to be able to self-correct; therefore, I indicate with a highlighter where an adjustment can be made. I don't "correct/grade" the papers until the typed version is completed.
- I prefer to have students write in class, so I can be certain they are not using Internet translators to create their cover letters.
- I refuse to play the human dictionary as I walk around the class, so I will only explain grammar or indicate if they have used a word correctly. They have to have something on their papers before I can help them improve.

CHAPTER 9

Author's Purpose for Readers' Choice

Micheline P. Plaskett

Ashland, Virginia

O ne of the goals of an elementary school librarian is to promote reading as a lifelong skill. When students come to a library, they expect to check out books to read and don't really think much about how that written word came to be on the page.

Students know they like to get specific information about their interests or be entertained with a captivating story. Many don't realize what genre they tend to gravitate toward, such as nonfiction or fiction—they just know they like it, hence they check it out.

My job is to help students understand the differences between the many genres of literature and develop an awareness of what they like to read, so they can try new genres to expand their horizons. Armed with insight, they may experiment with new choices to find new loves within the vast realm of literature.

An active way of developing this sense is to have readers turn into writers. Writers should base their creations with a specific purpose in mind. As the writer, what do I want from my readers? Do I want to persuade them, inform them, or entertain them? To help my students recall the three purposes of an author, I use the acronym PIE (persuade, inform, entertain). A circle divided into thirds and labeled P, I, and E serves as an apt illustration.

My fifth graders make an "Author's Purpose" brochure. They take a sheet of paper and fold it lengthwise into three even sections, as if they were folding it to go into a business-size envelope. On the cover, they title it, and on the three inside sections, they write the three different purposes.

I explain and give examples of the three types of author's purpose. For your lower-ability students, you may find it helpful to give a prompt for each purpose; however, whenever possible I prefer to give the students free rein so they may put their personal spin on each purpose, sifting through their strengths and weaknesses. They may surprise you—in fact, they may surprise themselves.

Do they notice they are more comfortable writing the purpose that reflects their personal reading preferences? Do they have some difficulty writing the purpose they have not personally read as much?

P: Persuade

It is not surprising that even my lowest-ability students can persuade their reader to buy a "Piggy bank shaped like a carrot because it comes with a free broccoli change machine and is the deal in all of Veggieville."

We who live in a capitalist society are bombarded with exposure to the powers of persuasion on television, radio, newspapers, magazines, snail mail, Internet, and in the marketplace! This is a good opportunity to teach critical viewing skills, not to mention bring out the "inventors" in the class.

I: Inform

Yes, students do have knowledge they can impart about people, places, and things. They may not realize just how informative they can be! A hobby, a sport, a passion, a mentor, or a pet could be within their personal realms of exposure, and this exercise forces knowledge transfer from life's experiences to their papers without the aid of investigative research.

The same young writer who teaches us about "George Washington, the first president of the United States . . ." or "How to make cereal . . ." with true and factual information may or may not have trouble switching gears from nonfiction to . . .

▩ E: Entertain

Fiction comes from the imagination, and the students will write stories that reflect their feelings, experiences, and that which they like to read: fantasy, science fiction, mysteries, realistic fiction, historical fiction, and others.

I remind my students that even though they are at liberty to write any fictional genre, they still need to follow the guidelines of story writing using story elements. And to entertain, the reader needs to be personally vested with the characters' plight evoking varying degrees of emotion.

We are truly entertained because we can relate to stories that begin with: "Benny Behemoth was a baseball player and he was not a very good one at that . . ." or "Betty the cow was a cow of wisdom and helped people solve their problems but there was one thing she knew: nothing . . ." or "Once upon a time there was a beautiful girl named Susie. . . ."

Upon completion of their Author's Purpose brochures, students may type their creations on the computer to reinforce today's technological demands, facilitate editing, and have even more fun. I help them to not only analyze their final work but also examine the thought processes involved in reaching a better understanding of what makes them tick and why.

Hopefully, this creative writing experience will initiate them to step out of their comfort zone by encouraging them to make innovative book choices and become more proficient and prolific writers.

CHAPTER 10

Punny Valentines

Creativity and Teamwork

Elizabeth F. Day

Mechanicville, New York

Practicing how to write friendly letters can sometimes become routine and unimaginative, so I decided to layer several ideas into one with a Punny Valentine project. My students explored the idea of puns and plays on words through various joke books, articles from magazines, and expressions that are used in everyday speech.

We categorized why some were considered puns and some were not, and the concept of pun was discovered. We then began making lists of people in our lives who perform certain jobs. We also made lists of cartoon characters or characters from literature or from pop culture. These lists included the local weatherman, professional sports players, the principal of our school, Dorothy from *The Wizard of Oz,* Harry Potter, and the Beatles.

For purposes of class demonstration, the students brainstormed ideas related to the local weatherman and what he might write in a "punny" way to someone whom he wanted to be his Valentine. The students had great fun coming up with lines like, "You stormed into my heart, you make my heart thunder with love, and I predict that you and I will be Valentines!" along with many other very clever ideas.

The class then chose four people from our class lists to brainstorm ideas about. Each group received a 12" × 18" piece of construction paper (placemat), which they divided into four sections, and in teams, brainstormed ideas about the four people. After this, each group had a chance to make a list of ideas for each of the four people we chose. The groups exchanged their placemats with other groups in the room so that the lists could be added to.

The results were creative and imaginative lists of ideas that could easily be transformed into puns and incorporated into Valentine friendly letters. Each student was asked to create at least one Punny Valentine friendly letter, and as the activity gained strength and speed, one group of boys asked if they could create a book of Valentines to send to their favorite sports stars.

Another group asked if they could write Valentine letters to our principal from various characters. We mailed some of our Punny Valentines to the students' sports heroes and we created a book of Punny Valentines for our principal, which we presented to him and he thoroughly enjoyed.

A new dimension had been added to our creative writing skills as my students had worked together, looked outside themselves, reached out to others, and had actively engaged in writing for a specific purpose. At year's end, many students chose their Valentine letters to be included in our class book titled "Our Favorite Pieces of Writing."

Helpful Tip

- Anticipate what activities can be potential "extenders" for a lesson for students who may not be able to take what was done to a higher level. Don't discount that artistic ability, or creative dramatics, might be a vehicle for students to go beyond the initial lesson. Students will often surprise you with what they are capable of and what they are good at—if you provide a pathway for them to show you.

CHAPTER 11

Being a Writer

A Tool for Improving Student Writing

Ganna Maymind

Morganville, New Jersey

O nce in a graduate class, I was asked to write something from my childhood. I sat there unsure of what to write about and how to organize my thoughts. After I wrote, I made lots of corrections and stared at my paper wondering if it was good enough. This made me think of my first graders' writing and how they feel when I give them a writing assignment and tell them to go and write. I thought that if they knew I felt the same way they did about writing, this could be a great point of connection between me and my students. It was also then that I realized that I cannot expect my students to write all the time if I am not a writer myself. I needed to show my students the kind of life that writers lead.

This started with getting a notebook and sitting down one night to write. The next day I brought in the notebook and shared it with my class. We were working on writing small moment stories (personal narratives), and I had written about running in a race. I thought you could hear a pin drop. They were so interested in my story and they clapped when I finished reading it. The next day, and every day that week, I read a different story from my notebook before the start of writing workshop. As I walked around, they seemed to enjoy their own writing more.

I show the children my writer's notebook. Before I share a piece, I discuss my thought process. I show them the words that I jot down, in case I don't want to forget something that happened that I later want to write about. I write what the students are writing. When working on small moment stories, or personal narratives, I share examples from my own life. When we are on our poetry unit, poems fill up my notebook. I share my struggles coming up with the topic and how I finally chose to write what I wrote about.

I once heard Donald Graves say that a writing conference means so much more when it is viewed as a conversation from one writer to another. That just couldn't be truer! Now when I walk around and pull up a chair next to a child to conference, I share about my own pieces. I can say, "Here is what I do when I am stuck," or "Sometimes to add more details, I use my five senses to help me."

I find it valuable to write about myself at the children's age. Since I teach first grade, my stories are often about when I rode my bike for the first time, spending time with my sister, or hugging my mom. I can see the room get very quiet, and their eyes and ears perk up, as I open up my writer's notebook and share about going skiing with my dad or opening up a gift from my friend.

No, you do not have to be the next John Grisham or Toni Morrison; you just have to write the way you expect your kids to. If I am working on having the children show—not tell—details in their stories, I'll make sure to write my story with those details. When working on good story endings, I'll write a story with a creative ending so that not all their stories end with, "And then I went to bed."

Showing children that you write outside of school also motivates them to do the same. After all, what first graders don't want to emulate their teacher? Slowly, they too want to have writer's notebooks at home and bring them in to share with the class. I make the biggest deal if a child brought in writing to share, not because it was homework, but because they wanted to write.

I am always amazed at my students' writing progress and attribute it to being a writer myself. Students need to understand that writing is not just doing an assignment at school, but taking your thoughts, fears, ideas, and experiences and getting them down on paper. It is not just words on a page, but a way to tell your personal story. I don't want the students to have my voice; I want to inspire them to have their own. As each student develops ownership and their unique style of writing, I know they are on their way to living the writer's life.

CHAPTER 12

Published Poems and Stories Treasured Forever

Pam Roller

Galveston, Indiana

For the last five years, I have made it my personal mission to have my second graders write poems for the Anthology of Poetry for Young Americans contest. It is hard work but well worth the effort. Poems have to be submitted to Anthology of Poetry, Inc., in Asheboro, North Carolina, by November 30 each year. Judges select poems from students in kindergarten through high school across the United States.

The poems are judged on content and whether they are age appropriate. Students, parents, and teachers are notified in February which poems have been selected for publication. The poems are published in hardbound books to be treasured for a lifetime.

It all began in the fall of 2001. It was the first time I had my students enter a poetry contest. We wrote poems monthly leading up to submitting the best ones for the poetry contest. I would put the monthly poems in spiral booklets and give each student a copy to keep. We sent in our entries.

In February 2002, every student in my class received a letter congratulating them for having a poem selected for publication! Wow! My students were now poets! A 2002 edition of the Anthology of Poetry for Young Americans was placed in our school library for students to check out. My students' poems have been selected for publication each year, including 2006.

It has been a way to culminate grammar skills and foster creativity in writing. I have students who are at risk, learning disabled, in special education, as well as those academically, emotionally, and socially challenged. I believe in accepting, respecting, and including every student.

It is amazing to see letters of congratulations going to parents of students who are mildly and moderately handicapped. It merely takes time and patience! The poems are not labeled "special needs" when they are sent to the Anthology of Poetry, Inc. The precious poems come out of the mouths of babes!

Every year when I have the students begin working on their poems for the contest, I hold up the hardbound editions from the previous years to show as examples. Many of the students recognize that their brothers and sisters have had poems published. This motivates them into becoming poets too.

In the spring of 2001, I had my class of second graders author and illustrate pages for a class book to be published through Studentreasures of Nationwide Learning in Topeka, Kansas. The book was titled *Moms Are Special!* This was a great way to culminate reading, writing, and grammar skills.

It also allowed students to be creative and have ownership of something they could cherish for years to come. They looked just like library books. A copy was purchased for our school library so it could be checked out. Kids are still checking out that book and letting me know they are reading it because my class authored and illustrated it.

Many children in my room could not afford to buy a book for their moms, so I bought each student a copy to give their moms for Mother's Day at a special breakfast in their honor on a Saturday morning in our classroom. The room was packed! Each child read and shared their pages.

One child's mom was under house arrest at the time, but she got permission to attend this special occasion. Another child's mom never showed any interest in her daughter's schoolwork, but she came to the Mother's Day breakfast to get the book.

My second graders have authored and illustrated class books since that time. In 2004, I invited each teacher in our school to do a class book with their students. We ended up with 20 published class books. We had a huge celebration for the students and teachers. Families were invited to attend. Our state senator was the master of ceremonies for the event.

A wall-size CD slide show of the books was shown, teachers and their students walked a red carpet to the song "One Moment in Time" by Whitney Houston, and they were presented with a star like those on the Walk of Fame in Hollywood.

A quilt was made featuring the 20 book covers, and it hangs in the foyer as you enter our school. Copies of all of these hardbound books are available for checkout in our school library.

Helpful Tips

- Students are eager to write when they have opportunities to share their own personal experiences. They get excited when they are allowed to be creative and use their imagination. Students are interested in projects when they have ownership.
- The published poems and stories I have mentioned in my article have built a sense of pride, confidence, and self-esteem in every student. The published work will be read for generations to come. Students look forward to having their work published, and we celebrate our writing annually!

CHAPTER 13

What's It Like to Be LD?

Peter W. Riffle

W. Lawn, Pennsylvania

W hy is it so very difficult to inspire learning-disabled kids to put forth effort in reading and writing classes? Teachers create thought-provoking and inspiring lessons that far too often meet with little or marginal success. Why? Stop and consider what it must be like to be a learning-disabled person. Actually, it is virtually impossible to imagine this lifelong challenge if you haven't "walked in these shoes."

I know what it's like because I've suffered from this esteem-shattering condition my entire life, but trying to explain it to normal learners is difficult. When lecturing to college students, I use the following two methods to illustrate what it's like to be an LD child in school. These two exercises drive home the feelings of learning-disabled kids faster and more efficiently than any lecture ever given.

I always begin each session with lighthearted bantering with the students. A big deal is made about who in the lecture hall can follow directions. Naturally, being university students, they can all follow directions perfectly! Each student is given a sealed envelope and instructed not to open it until told to do so. I then ask everyone to stand.

The last directive I give is to open the envelope, read the enclosed passage, and sit down when they know exactly what it says. Everyone sits down quickly, except for five kids who stand there bewildered, wondering why everyone read it so quickly and they couldn't.

In order to make them feel even more uncomfortable, I say things such as, "Come on, this is so simple," or "Stop clowning around; we can't go on with the lesson until you finish this easy assignment." Why could everyone except these five college students understand what was in the envelope? After all, each person had only the first two lines of "Mary Had a Little Lamb" typed on a piece of paper.

Well—those five had the same two lines, but theirs were written in Russian! At this point I say, "How did you like it?" Those left standing admitted feeling foolish and embarrassed in front of their classmates. Learning-disabled students go through this discomfiture every day of their lives in school, so it is no wonder why they hate school.

Another way to describe the life of an LD kid in school is to use my "T-ball" story. I will ask a non-athletic-looking student from the audience to come stand by me. Since most kids have played T-ball at some time in their lives, I begin relating coaching stories about teaching seven- and eight-year-olds the finer points of T-ball.

While looking at my role-playing participant, I give the students the following scenario: You are now part of a T-ball team, and you play a game every day. Each one of your teammates is allowed to hit off of the "T" and run the bases. When it's your turn to bat, the "T" is removed, and you must hit one of Nolan Ryan's 95-mph fastballs.

You strike out every time, and your coach demands to know why you can't get a hit. Your fellow players begin to make fun of you. You go home and tell your parents you want to quit the team, but you're told that is not an option. This endless game goes on day after day for years. You still can't quit, and you never experience success. Observing the nodding heads in the audience, I sense that some understanding of the plight of the learning-disabled child has begun to take place.

CHAPTER 14

Think—Talk—Write

Rosemary Fryer

Vancouver, Washington

*A*aron literally dropped into my classroom from the world of special education. His mother insisted that Aaron needed the stimulation of regular education; from her perspective, Aaron coasted through his classes without gaining the skills she felt Aaron needed to succeed in life.

So, he appeared in class, dazed, confused, and scared, kicked out of his comfortable cocoon, thrust into the cruelty of a mainstream class. For the first three weeks, Aaron cried every day, frustrated by the pace of the class and the seemingly overwhelming demands on his abilities. Seeking some help, I contacted his ninth-grade special education teacher. He assumed the I-told-you-so position: I told you Aaron didn't belong in regular education classes; I told you he read at the fifth-grade level; I told you he didn't write well; I told you Aaron was slow.

I asked for a conference with Aaron's mother. I explained Aaron's dismay and his sadness. Launching into a tirade on special education and the insensitivity and dismissiveness of regular education teachers toward students like Aaron, she remained steadfast—Aaron would stay in my English class and in my teaching partners' classes. She had tossed the gauntlet, issued the challenge—teach my son.

I made a plan. First, I had to reduce Aaron's anxiety. Aaron's frustration stemmed from his inability to keep up with the pace of the class. The transition from one activity to the next proved too daunting for him. Since articulating his thinking from mind to ink produced in Aaron considerable angst, I introduced him to "talk-write." I assigned Aaron "talk-write" partners.

These partners helped Aaron by recording his thoughts as he spoke them. His partners wrote his thinking for journal prompts, group conversations, and posters. In Aaron's support class, his teacher and staff assistant copied the same technique so he could brainstorm ideas for essays and reports.

Besides the talk-writing, I modeled each step of every assignment for Aaron and for all my students. Making my thinking transparent, I crafted each part so he could see the expectations and refer to an example. From seeing, Aaron launched to doing, as did the rest of my students. My modeling transferred power to Aaron, the power of understanding.

After about four weeks of talk-writing and modeling, Aaron relaxed. He began to feel more confident academically, and he trusted me that I would not abandon him but support him. With that confidence and trust, he took the initiative. Instead of crying, he figured out plans to accomplish assignments. Many times, Aaron made appointments with me after school; together we chunked the big task into manageable pieces, assigning deadlines for each chunk.

Then we would talk-write; he talked and I wrote, brainstorming ideas for his science report or history essay, even his English papers. During the course of the talk-write, I would ask him questions, not only about ideas but also about organization and elaboration. I discussed my progress on the task, sharing my ideas.

When Aaron wrote his essay about Iago from Shakespeare's *Othello,* he revealed the depth of his insight into the motivations of this sinister character. Aaron was not the same Aaron of early September.

Recently, one of Aaron's teachers used him as an example of a student who, challenged by the subject, demonstrated self-reliance by seeking extra assistance to complete his work. I smiled to myself, happy that Aaron's transformation is permanent and that I accepted his mother's challenge three years ago.

Helpful Tips

- *Set a Purpose.* Give students the reasons for the work.
- *Set Goals.* State the targets students will achieve.
- *Model.* Make your thinking transparent; show students how.

CHAPTER 15

The "Art" of Merging Descriptive and Narrative Writing

Sharon Andrews

Sioux Falls, South Dakota

As educators know, each year is different, each classroom is different, each individual is different, and we are not always sure that our best-laid plans will achieve the desired outcomes. The following provides an account of my experiences with teaching writing, including a description of some general strategies, problems that were encountered with a particular class of students, and adjustments in the teaching plan that were made to compensate for this particular group.

The beginning of the school year brings a new classroom of eager students with many new worlds to explore, and it is a wonderful time to engage all their senses through descriptive writing. To facilitate their ideas for writing, I bring in something for the children to experience, such as a popular food like popcorn. First, the students are asked to describe how the popcorn looks, smells, tastes, feels, and sounds as it is popping. Then we discuss descriptive words such as adjectives and adverbs, and the differences between strong and weak verbs.

Later we move on to describe other things, such as a bedroom or a favorite person. Finally, through these exercises, the students improve their use of word choice and write beautiful descriptive paragraphs. These activities and experiences excite students about descriptive writing and serve as a microcosm for challenges in descriptive writing throughout the year.

During the second quarter, the objectives are expanded as I progress on to narrative writing. I have found that most children love to write stories, and the excitement of being more descriptive as an integral part of their writing style provides momentum to the students' attitude toward the endeavors.

Techniques involved in the narrative writing assignments include class discussions toward identifying elements of a good narrative and the use of graphic organizers to plan out the stories. After the students have spent several days working on their first narratives, I am always anxious to read the initial drafts.

Following the discovery of how famous authors manage writing exciting plots and beautifully detailed paragraphs, I asked the students to review their own drafts to locate areas that require more descriptive detail and, when necessary, prompted students with specific questions for more specific description. As they compared their own descriptive writing with that of famous authors, their sensitivity and awareness of the concept were improved.

Finally, in consideration of various learning styles and to further enhance the descriptive aspect of writing, I showed the class Norman Rockwell's painting *The Runaway*. This famous painting shows a police officer and a boy sitting on stools at a diner.

The two are talking as the waiter looks on, and apparently the boy has run away from home because there is a knapsack on the floor by his side. I enjoyed using this particular painting because almost all children can relate to having thoughts of running away at one time or another.

For this activity, I displayed the painting at the front of the classroom and also distributed smaller copies to each student. I first asked the students to examine the picture individually for a few moments, jotting down in their writer's notebooks any features or details that they noticed, thus providing an inventory for use in descriptive writing.

The students' individual observations were shared with the rest of the class and displayed on the overhead projector. Cooperatively, the entire class expanded the inventory of observations for descriptive writing by including particular words and phrases to describe details in the scene. After the inventory was complete, the students were instructed to write a descriptive paragraph using some of the words and phrases that were previously recorded. Again, the paragraphs were full of images and details that repainted the picture with words.

Now it was time once again to approach the difficult transition of merging the descriptive snapshots with the plot of the story and therefore provide motion and momentum to the descriptive scenes.

The students were asked to do what all kids love to do—write a story about what they think happened in the picture, including what may have happened from when the policeman first found the boy, what the action in the picture portrayed, and to complete the action by describing what happened thereafter. Further, while most children would choose to write from the boy's point of view, I also encouraged them to write from the perspective of another character, such as the police officer or the diner clerk.

Finally, after the narratives were written, I asked the students to find places in their stories where more description would fit nicely, look at the descriptive paragraphs that they had previously written, and insert them as descriptive snapshots in their stories.

Helpful Tips

- Teach descriptive writing before teaching narratives. The narratives will be more interesting with nicely written descriptions interspersed.
- Model good descriptive writing for your students. Students learn a lot by watching others write and observing the thought processes involved.
- Find well-written passages from famous authors. Read these passages to the class while noting how the authors merge the plot with description. Then have the students find examples from their favorite authors to share with the class.

(Continued)

Helpful Tips (Continued)

- After the students write a narrative, ask the students to find places in their stories to add descriptive snapshots. Tell them that this is a necessary part of revising a story.
- Always find positive things to say about each child's writing. I always talk about the positive aspects of the writing before giving constructive suggestions.

CHAPTER 16

Writing the Wrongs

A Middle School Student Unravels the Knots of Her Life Through Writing

Susan Okeson

Chugiak, Alaska

*A*s educators, we always find students who touch our hearts; one of my most touching cases centers around a girl named Sandy. Sandy was a first grader when I first became the principal of her elementary school. Sandy was small for her age and considerably behind academically; however, she had a bright smile and a heart of pure gold. She was a student who did everything with kindness and compassion.

Even more remarkable is that Sandy was kind and generous despite her home life, which was one of the most distressing I'd ever seen. Sandy's dad had fathered nine children with three different women, two of whom were in and out of prison frequently.

For reasons I will never be able to fathom, this man maintained full custody of these children—although they spent short amounts of time in various foster homes as the Office of Children's Services investigated and applied consequences to Sandy's father. Four of the nine younger siblings attended my elementary school, along with Sandy.

Over the next four years, I kept a close eye on Sandy's progress and watched her grow and learn under the tutelage of her classroom teachers, our resource teachers, teacher aides, and parent volunteers. While she remained behind academically, the progress she made was consistent, albeit slow, and I still marvel at her perseverance and the huge smile she would offer when praised for a job well done.

In March of my fourth year, medical reasons necessitated that I take the rest of the school year off to undergo treatment. In July, Sandy's father, Tim, called me at home and said that Sandy's mother was trying to get custody of her. Tim was teary and said, "She's my best kid . . . I can't lose her." He told me he needed a letter from me that he could share with the court about how well he was doing as a father.

In good conscience, I could not write a letter affirming his parenting skills, but I was also concerned about the traits of a mother who, until two months earlier, had been nonexistent in her little girl's life. I didn't see or hear from Sandy for four years. She did not return to school in the fall, and I made it back to school in November. The next year, I moved to a school nearer my home. Then, after four years of only wondering about Sandy's circumstances, I suddenly saw Sandy's family being discussed on every television news channel. The news was covering a story of an intoxicated young man who had stolen a car, run a red light, and killed a man in a collision.

This intoxicated car thief was Sandy's older brother, one of the few siblings I did not know from their neighborhood school. I immediately thought of Sandy and hoped she was in foster care far away from all the media coverage. She was not.

My husband, Mark, an assistant principal at a high school in a neighboring school district, came home that day and said that Sandy's school counselor (she was now 13 and attending a local middle school) had called him because Sandy was trying to find me.

The counselor asked Mark if Sandy could have our phone numbers, telling us that Sandy had talked fondly of time spent with us years ago, and wanted to know if it was okay to release our phone numbers. Mark gave the counselor all our numbers, and the next afternoon Sandy called my house. Sandy's mother had gotten custody soon after her father had contacted me four years earlier, and she was now living not too far from my house. Sandy said that she was allowed to see her dad and siblings that weekend, and she wanted to know if we could get together and have dinner Saturday night.

Mark and I picked up Sandy and two of her older siblings and took them out for a dinner together. What an enlightening experience for us all! Sandy's brother was now a sophomore and said he was trying to get his grades up so he could play basketball next fall. I gave them my e-mail address and we all promised to keep in touch. Sandy's voice is so clearly evident in her e-mails to me and her writing is so touching that oftentimes I cry. Sandy writes volumes, punctuated with the appropriate conventions as well as smiley faces, hearts, and thumbs-up symbols—as only a 13-year-old can do. I am so impressed with her writing ability, and told her this recently.

She responded with a look of embarrassment and shyly said, "I write what I hear in my heart." I told her that one of my particular favorite letters reads, "I am so glad that you are back in my life now. It is like I am finding pieces of my life and gluing them all back together. Kinda like a picture of my life where the faces of people I love were torn out a long time ago and I am mending it and putting the faces back around me." I also responded with a "me too," when she ended an e-mail with, "I just want you to know that you mean a lot to my heart and I will never, ever forget you."

While graduating seniors will oftentimes publicly thank a high school teacher, it is important not to forget the groundwork that has been laid by the earlier childhood educators. Sandy says she does not explicitly remember the day she learned to write (I tell her that's because writing is a process), but she does recall certain favorite writing activities she participated in during elementary school.

Sandy cited writer's workshop, journaling, author's tea, and reading her work to the principal as having the most impact. She also said that she wouldn't be the writer she is without the use of a computer, for editing purposes, and is glad that she learned how to type in fifth grade.

CHAPTER 17

Finding the Time to Write in Your Language Arts Curriculum

Stacy Gardner Dibble

Worthington, Minnesota

G reat basketball players spend countless hours shooting hoops. The best hockey players grow up skating on the ice. Likewise, excellent math students spend lots of time solving math problems, and accomplished readers have read their way through most libraries. However, when it comes to writing, it appears that our students do not spend much time practicing the skill of writing.

When I went back to school to get my master's degree, I spent about six months looking at the research to find the best ways to improve student writing. The answer that I found after extensive searching was actually quite simple. If you want students to be better writers, they need to do one easy task: write. In today's language arts classrooms, students actually do very little writing. Grammar lessons consist of underlining, filling in the blanks, and drawing circles around words.

Writing lessons involve writing to a prompt that may or may not inspire them to write at all. Revision means teachers gutting students' papers with a bright red pen to the point that they no longer have any vested interest in the writing that they did; they merely want the rough draft back so they can copy what the teacher wrote on it and hand it in to get it off their desks.

I felt compelled to find a way for my students to spend that 15 minutes a night engaged in writing activities that would be interesting, fun, and challenging enough to keep them writing. I found three strategies that ensure that my students are getting at least 15 minutes of writing time 4 or more days a week. They are literacy bags, technology, and journal writing.

A literacy bag includes a picture book or two, questions that address the higher-order thinking skills, and writing projects that go with each story, such as letter writing, thank-you notes, journal entries, diaries, list making, and report writing. Currently I have assigned one literacy bag a month. Every student takes it home, and they have one week to complete the activities in each unit. I have differentiated the activities and questions so that if I have a student with special needs, I can adapt the bag to make it appropriate. The students have enjoyed the book selections and the writing activities that go with them.

Technology is an area that we do not often think of as a necessary component of a language arts curriculum. I have found that using technology is a must if I want to improve the writing skills of my students. Remember that our goal is to get students to spend more time writing so that it becomes more natural for them. One of the most obvious ways that technology can improve writing is in the area of time.

With the use of spelling and grammar checks, the ability to have research at the students' fingertips, and the ease of using a personal computer to save, type, and edit a piece of writing, the computer can save volumes of time. Trying to incorporate technology into my plan to get students writing after school hours was not going to be an easy task. I work in a very poor district, and many of our families do not have access to technology. I was awarded a $2,000 grant and I used that money to purchase six AlphaSmart computers. The AlphaSmart is a portable word-processing keyboard that students can use to type their writing projects.

Each AlphaSmart has eight different files on which they can store their work. The AlphaSmart also has a Spanish/English dictionary that is very helpful to the students in my classroom who do not speak English, or whose parents cannot help them at home because they do not speak English. Students return the "computer" to me and I am able to plug it into my computer, open up a file, and hit Send. It will automatically send me a student's writing. I can then easily edit their writing and print it.

However, the most effective prompt I ever gave my students was the freedom to allow them to journal about whatever they want! My students are required to journal 4 days a week, for 15 minutes at a time. They are assigned specific days to return their journals to me so I don't have all 25 journals to read coming in on the same day.

In the past, I required students to keep journals for a variety of reasons, and I always gave up on them. Journaling is a habit. As the classroom teacher, you really need to be a consistent model in order to get your students into that habit. The entire month of September, I have students do all their journaling during class time. I model everything, including how I want them to record the date, the time they start journaling, and the time they stop journaling. While they are writing, I write as well, and then I share my journal with them.

Once a week, I read their journal entries and write very brief comments to them about what I have read. I never "correct" a student's journal in any way. If I did, they would start editing their writing, and this would not help them learn to get their thoughts down on the paper first. I feel privileged to read my students' journals. It is a very powerful way to get students writing, but it also helps them to make the connection that what they have to say in writing is important.

CHAPTER 18

We Write, You Read, We All Win for Literacy!

Carly Pumphrey

Falling Waters, West Virginia

D o you struggle with getting your students to write? Does your principal want you to involve the community in your classroom? Then it is time for you to create a classroom newsletter written by your students to share with your community! You will simply need a computer with publishing software (such as Microsoft Publisher), a digital camera, a printer, and students who want to write for a purpose.

At the beginning of the project, I model writing for my students. I always begin by making a story web with the topic in the middle circle and three to four details about the topic attached to the circle. I model using the web to write four sentences about the topic. Then we edit the writing together. As a first-grade teacher, I concentrate mostly on capital letters and punctuation. As the year goes on, we edit for details and variety of word choice. This project could easily be adjusted to any grade level by simply addressing your grade level's writing standards.

My first-grade students practice writing every day. We choose to write about school events, such as the first-grade Thanksgiving Feast, Fall Festival, our lessons on patterns, and so on. The students find these things very easy to write about, because they have experienced them. I publish the newsletter each month and try to include topics related to each month.

I always take pictures of all these events. The pictures help prompt the students to write and are great additions to the newsletter. I also add clip art to the newsletter when a digital picture is not available. The students love to choose their own clip art pictures to add to their writings.

The students want to share the information about the events from school with the community, the community wants to learn about the events going on in the school, and the students get lots of practice writing in the process. This makes *We Write, You Read, We All Win for Literacy* a Win-Win project!

Helpful Tips

- Choose a simple template for your newsletter at the beginning of the year and just cut and paste the students' writing into the template. I simply did a two-sided, one-page template for my first graders.
- Take pictures of all events and classroom activities. They could prompt a writing project you would not otherwise have planned.
- Choose a certain number of student writings to be included in the newsletter. Keep track of the students whose writing is included each month, so that all students will be included throughout the year.
- Allow the more advanced students to write for the newsletter at the beginning of the year, and allow the struggling writers to practice throughout the year and publish toward the end.
- Include a variety of writing. Poems and "how-to" stories are easier for struggling writers.
- Copy enough newsletters to send home with each student in the school and also to place in community areas, such as doctors' offices, banks, and so on.
- Print color copies of the newsletter and place them in a clear protective sleeve to add to your classroom library. The students love reading their own writings and sharing them with classmates!

CHAPTER 19

"Small Moment" Stories

A Way to Improve Student Writing

Ganna Maymind

Morganville, New Jersey

I remember coming back to school in January a few years ago, refreshed following our winter break. After sitting in a circle and sharing some things we did over break, I asked my first graders to take out their journals and start writing. I set the timer and put on a classical music CD, to get the kids back into our writing routine.

As I walked around, I was shocked to see only a couple of sentences on the students' pages. We had just spent all morning sharing stories and little adventures about what they did, yet when it came time to write, I saw a few simple sentences and a picture. Why were they not writing everything they shared? I know the stories were in their heads, yet how would I help the students relocate the stories from their minds onto paper? I had to come up with a better way to approach writing instruction in my first-grade classroom.

After reading various books by Graves, Calkins, and countless others, something seemed to stand out: a "small moment" story. Instead of asking children to write about their whole winter break, I would ask them to pick one event, one moment, and write only about that. It seemed to make sense, so I embarked on my journey to improving the way I taught writing.

I gathered the children on the rug, as I usually do for writing work-shop, and told them we were going to start something new in writing. Instead of writing everything about their weekends, vacations, or holidays, we would zoom in, just as photographers do, on only one part. I modeled a lot of my own stories to show them what it sounded like. Then I asked them to close their eyes and picture just one moment, one event.

As I taught the children how to write small moments, we read a lot of quality literature that exemplifies small moments. My favorite is *Shortcut* by Donald Crews. In this story, it is clear that Donald Crews, instead of writing about his whole summer at his grandmother's house, chose to zoom in on one part. Other favorite authors include Ezra Jack Keats, Vera Williams, Cynthia Rylant, Angela Johnson, and Patricia Polacco.

I noticed that some children were still having trouble "stretching" their stories out. So I show them how using five fingers to tell their story can help. I model starting with the thumb and continuing through to the last finger, saying a sentence as I hold up each finger. As I get to the middle finger, I always say: "It's the middle of my story so I better finish up." I noticed that stories started to take up a whole page, rather than a few sentences. Zooming in on one part allowed the children's stories to go beyond favorite toys and video games and were instead about scoring a soccer goal, hugging their grandmother, or eating an ice-cream sundae.

We also discussed telling not only the outside story but the inside story, meaning that the students write not only what happened but how they felt. We used phrases such as "I thought," "I noticed," "I felt," and "I wondered." This is also the point where stories started to have better endings, such as with a feeling or a question, rather than the famous "and then we went home" that I had often seen my students write.

I only wish I knew this "small moment" technique sooner. I think it really gives kids a way to approach writing that is not threatening. Instead, it is a manageable way that gives even the most struggling writers a way to enjoy writing. At the end of that year, everyone, myself included, looked forward to writing time. Most of all, it made the children want to write during their free time and even after the year was over.

Helpful Tips

- I made sure to model a lot for the kids what a small moment story looks like. This meant looking for small moments in my own life and sharing these with the children. They loved getting to know me as a person. Another way to let students hear quality writing is to read their classmates' writing (that you have prechosen). I often ask a child to read his or her story and ask the class to notice certain things that the child did well, such as adding lots of details or feelings. This empowers children, since they hear someone in their own class writing so well.
- I also found it helpful to write small moment stories together. We would pick an experience we all had together, such as a fire drill, an assembly, or going to art class. I would ask them to picture this story in their heads and share a version with their partners. Then we would write a small moment story together, having the children share what sentence they think should go next.
- For example, this year after our Halloween party, we wrote a class piece on decorating pumpkins. It was easy for them to see my thought process about how the story went yet also gave them a chance to listen to each other.

CHAPTER 20

Writing in the Palm of Your Hand

Carla Hurchalla

Salisbury, Maryland

Recently, we have begun using handheld computers for writing activities. Classes of students are using them from first grade through eighth grade. We have found that the quality of work that the students are producing is superior to what they produce with paper and pencil. Students are given a handheld computer and a keyboard. They learn where the keys are very quickly and are more apt to include rich language.

Because the writing process is so involved, students take more time when they are using the handheld computers because they recognize the fact that they won't have to rewrite the entire piece in order to revise and strengthen it. Students also share what they have written with their peers very easily through beaming.

Students create e-books that they beam to each other. This way, everyone in a class receives everyone else's e-books. This provides a real audience for the student work, and students are proud of their finished pieces. Parents are also impressed when they see their children using this technology to create quality work.

Helpful Tip

- If handheld computers are not available in your area, any type of computer will work. Students love to type their stories and will spend a great deal of time revising and making sure the finished product is a strong piece that others would want to read.

CHAPTER 21

Walking the Introduction

Eric Stemle

Evanston, Wyoming

My purple pen inked yet another marginal note to Ethan, one of my sophomore writers, and I hoped my script was not only legible but somehow hid my growing frustration. My comments centered on the lack of organization found in the essay's introduction, a problem I was finding in a majority of the papers I had read that morning. The closest thing I could find to a thesis opened the first paragraph, and what followed was a list of ideas to be covered all too briefly in the body of the argument.

Despite our practice a few days before, Ethan and a good number of his classmates seemed to have reverted to previous learning. Whether they were confusing the structure of an introduction with that of other paragraphs or perhaps remembering how they were instructed by teachers years before, my kids were struggling mightily with an abstraction with their feet firmly set in the concrete. We had a problem.

Determined to help my kids learn expository format, I assessed my instructional methods. I had provided the class with a set of guidelines for writing introductions, given them a chance to write intros with a partner, and showed them samples from previous classes. They had seemed to grasp the basic structure in these activities, yet when the essays came in, my pen was busy with reminders.

The effort seemed about right—there was evidence that the kids had devoted time and thought to producing the best writing they could muster—so the answer must lie with me. I decided that the task required conceptual thinking, which most of my students were having a tough time achieving. Somehow I had to find a way to move them from the concrete level of following a guideline sheet to the abstract level of creating a funneled introduction to a viable thesis with no prompting. It was clear that in order for Ethan and company to succeed, they literally had to get their feet moving.

The next day I gathered my class within one side of our circle of desks for a moving exercise in introduction writing. One thing I knew about my reluctant writers was that they preferred being out of their seats, and if they could be milling around and talking at the same time, they would be even happier. Standing in the middle of the circle, I announced a topic: cars. I held up a dictionary and asked for a volunteer to define car for the class. There was a pause lasting maybe 10 seconds before Robbie stepped forward, took the Webster's from my hand, and seconds later read aloud, "A vehicle moving on wheels." I thanked him for his initiative and asked him to step to the side opposite the rest of the class.

"All right," I said, "we need someone to come to the center and give us an example of a car." A shorter hesitation this time, and Becka danced to the middle.

"Chevy," she said with a smile.

"Another example?" I asked as I motioned her to join Robbie.

Kayce walked to the center and said, "Ford."

Before the words were out of my mouth, Marty sauntered to the middle. "Ferrari," he said, eyes growing wide.

"All right," I said, "now we need a volunteer to state an opinion about cars."

Dillon looked as though he couldn't wait to share. He ran to the center of the circle and nearly shouted, "Cars are the coolest!"

"Okay," I said. "What we have here is the makings of an essay introduction. It's not ready yet, but we have the ingredients for sure." I asked the five to arrange themselves in order of presentation for an introduction and reminded them to use a complete sentence when reprising each part. Within seconds the kids arranged themselves into a straight line and announced their team introduction:

"A car is a vehicle that moves on wheels."

"One kind of car is a Chevy."

"Ford is a kind of car, too."

"Dude, Ferraris are sweet cars."

"Cars are the coolest!"

We began another introduction on the topic of movies, and the play continued until every student had the chance to contribute to an introduction. The kids seemed to enjoy the exercise, but I knew there was more to accomplish. The next day, as class began, Ethan asked if we could "write" more introductions. I smiled and told him that was the plan for the day. This time we added a step. When each group finished their announcement, I asked them to write the paragraph in their notebooks. I encouraged them to include transitions between sentences to ease the flow.

The following day, I gave the kids a list of topics from which to choose and had them write their own introductions. As I went from desk to desk, I had the opportunity to see how much each writer had learned. Some still wrote in choppy sentences, but all seemed to have the idea of the funnel. What had been born of frustration became the secret to helping kids think conceptually. Students don't suddenly think abstractly because we ask them to.

Rather, we must lead them by taking them step-by-step from a hands-on experience to a blending of the physical and the mental and finally to more sophisticated tasks. When the next essays came in, my purple comments were celebratory in nature. The kids had finally clicked with the structure of an introduction. Sure, they had to learn various ways of opening, to develop depth, but the basic foundation had been laid. Now if only they could write a good body paragraph. . . .

Helpful Tips

- One thing to keep in mind in teaching writing is the tendency for students to revert to their first experience with an element of composition. The key to avoiding this is to give kids the big picture before concentrating on an aspect to practice. For instance, if I teach my students that they can start an introduction by defining a topic, some writers will continue to do that exclusively. Instead, I let them know from the outset that there are a number of ways to open an essay, and that we'll be exploring each one in time to provide them with a menu of choices.

- Another consideration in helping kids develop writing concepts is to spread out each step. I try to schedule each stage a day or two apart to give the kids time to assimilate the information. Once they have the confidence of accomplishing one part, they seem to accept the next phase more readily. Finally, I never let my students get the impression that I am discouraged with their writing. Sure, if they could see me grading their papers at home, they might get a sense of my disappointment with slow progress, but in class or in conference, I exude hope and confidence in their abilities. I know of no better way to inspire.

CHAPTER 22

Writing Tools for the First-Grade Classroom

Nikki Salvatico

Malvern, Pennsylvania

W riting in the first-grade setting works hand in hand with teaching children how to read. Part of teaching writing in the first-grade setting is to supply the children with the necessary tools they will need to work independently and produce an acceptable final product. Referencing resources is a life skill that reinforces problem solving. For my first graders, becoming readers and writers allows me to begin that referencing process in a more sophisticated yet developmentally appropriate manner.

I provide my students with a writing handbook and writing checklist that will allow them to work more independently. They can use these tools as they produce their work and then again as they edit. It allows the students to begin thinking about their own writing. It opens up opportunities to make changes so the reader will feel the story as the students want it told.

The writing handbook is usually used during the writing process until the final draft is composed. (Please note: Final drafts are not done for each writing piece my students construct; most final drafts are for assessment purposes only.) This handbook allows students to have a few ideas to pull from or to help spark new ideas. It allows students to make the handbook their own by leaving space for additional ideas. It also allows students to work independently.

The writing checklist is usually used when the student's rough draft is complete. This checklist is to help create "editors" out of each student. It provides guidelines that support the student in the editing process. There are two checklists to complete. One is "checking for" the possible mistakes, the other is to state that the mistakes found were "fixed." I have often found that children will check off an item just because they read their paper yet end up never fixing the mistakes; therefore, I have added the "fixed" column to help decrease that habit.

The checklist also includes a section where the students are to read their writing to themselves using our handmade PVC piping phones. The phones allow a child to read their story, speaking into one end of the phone and hearing their voice from the other end of the phone. This helps to catch mistakes they would not normally catch by reading it silently. The other important section is to have a friend read the piece to the writer. This will also help to catch those mistakes they may not read incorrectly because it is their own work and they do not "see" the mistake.

I have found that this concrete, sequential, multistep process in editing allows fewer mistakes to appear on the final draft, as well as helping my writers become better readers and readers become better writers!

Helpful Tip

■ Over the past seven years teaching first grade, I have found that allowing your children to write on a topic of their choice, as well as using larger chart paper and markers, has increased not only the children's writing ability but also their enthusiasm for writing. I often have to tell them to stop because it is time to go home. That to me is amazing!

CHAPTER 23

Revitalize Your Teaching Through Collaboration and Integration

Mary Merrill
Barbara Sabin

Bethel, Maine

I n order to provide an appropriate and challenging education for our kindergarten students, it is important to constantly review the curriculum and update our lessons. At the beginning of each year, we evaluate past lessons, review the curriculum, and realign our program. In an effort to remain creative and enthusiastic about teaching, we brainstorm, strategize, and implement new ideas as a team. An example of this collaboration is the creation of our theme-related technology project.

Through team teaching, we discovered that the demands of mandates and assessments were not as overwhelming as we first thought but were actually achievable. The technology project that we created, using both the multifaceted HyperStudio and the engaging Kidspiration programs, resulted in a high level of achievement. This task included researching an ocean creature, its habitat, food sources, and characteristics using Web booklets, the Internet, and literature.

Here's what the project involved:

- Creating an informational web using the Kidspiration program
- Using the Web to create a written report about the ocean creature
- Creating "stacks" in the HyperStudio program
- Inserting pictures from the Internet
- Drawing and inserting illustrations from the Paint program to accompany the text
- Developing an author page and table of contents
- Assembling the above components into a book
- Sharing the end result with classmates and family

All these steps were completed with the help of community volunteers, school personnel, upper-class computer buddies, and the classroom teachers. Using volunteers, technology, and a hands-on approach to learning motivates students to achieve a greater understanding of the learning process along with the standards required in our curriculum, as well as accommodating the varied learning styles of children. In conclusion, by collaborating as colleagues, utilizing volunteers, implementing resources, and taking risks, we creatively meet the requirements of the ever-evolving state and local mandates.

CHAPTER 24

Lifesaving Technique

Vicki Goldsmith

Des Moines, Iowa

Ten years ago, after teaching college writing courses for several years, I got a job teaching high school Advanced Placement (AP) Literature and Composition. I was used to having several office hours a week and personal conferences with students to discuss their writing. Out of frustration that there was no way to have personal time with 108 students in a high school, I began what was to become a lifesaving technique: I gave each student a cassette tape to hand in with each major paper, and I responded to the assignment verbally.

The advantages were a surprise to me. I could say 10 times more in 15 minutes than I could write in that time. I had to go beyond the usual dozen, clichéd comments and address the paper individually. I had time to explain constructions and problems instead of simply writing "passive voice" in the margin. My tone of voice let students know my attitude, something they couldn't tell from written comments.

No one could skip the commentary and just look at the grade, since by the time the grade was announced at the end of the taping, the writer knew exactly where it came from—though occasionally a student would go out to his car at lunch and fast-forward the tape to the grade! In 10 years, I had not a single complaint about a grade, but many students chose to rewrite papers, because they knew exactly what needed to be done to improve the work.

I encouraged submitting rewritten pieces but required a brief written explanation of the corrections. Since I was talking to just one person, I could add personal comments I didn't have time for in class, such as, "Your ideas are stunning, but you are silent in class; practice getting ready for college courses by nudging your way into class discussion." Or "You did a marvelous job in the concert last week." Although taping the comments for the papers took as long or longer than writing responses, I found the grading much less stressful. I got up early in the morning and taped while the world was silent.

Once I started to talk, I was fully focused on that paper. Students waited eagerly to get their papers back, and many said they felt they were really learning to write for the first time because the responses were thorough. It is easy, when you have too much paperwork, to skim over the excellent papers and simply write, "Good work." An A student seldom complains about too little feedback. These tapes guaranteed that I gave good students as much response as those who needed corrections and reworking.

I started every paper with positive commentary, then told students, even those with A's, what to work on. Many parents listened to their kids' taped comments (with permission, of course) and came to parent conferences knowing exactly what their children were working on. They raved about the tapes, since they knew that their kids were not just numbers in a crowd. Some students, especially shy ones, taped commentaries back to me and began a dialogue—in some ways, this was better than a conference.

The disadvantages of the system are few. Weak papers sometimes take longer than 15 minutes, but I find that students who want to learn appreciate the effort. My living room floor is usually covered with dozens of manila folders, and almost every day I carry bags and bags of papers around; however, I would never go back to written responses.

CHAPTER 25

Teaching Writing With an Eclectic Approach Across the Curriculum

C. Joyce Taylor

Fort Smith, Arkansas

The crux of my writing curriculum is based on the English Language Arts Curriculum Framework of the Arkansas Department of Education. The A+ Schools Network's philosophy, teaching across the curriculum, and using a variety of writing approaches drive my teaching methodology.

Arkansas sixth-grade standards for teaching writing are two-pronged. First, writing: Different genres of writing—narrative, expository, and descriptive—are practiced. Specific skills—good leads and conclusions, for example—and figurative language, such as similes, metaphors, onomatopoeia, and personification, are addressed. Poetry is an integral part of my writing program. Content and style are stressed.

Second, English and language arts: Sentence formation, usage, and mechanics are the three language categories in which the Arkansas Comprehensive Testing, Assessment, and Accountability Program (ACTAAP) tests students. Therefore, parts of speech and specific skills such as subject-verb agreement are taught.

A lot of emphasis is placed on sentence formation—writing a variety of sentences, in kind and length, and beginning sentences in different ways, with adjectives, prepositional phrases, and so on. Sentence revision, by combining parts or whole sentences, is an expectation.

Cook School has been accepted as part of the A+ Schools Network, a North Carolina program that embraces the fine arts and thematic teaching that incorporates Dr. Howard Gardner's theory of multiple intelligences, a theory I have believed in and implemented to various degrees throughout my teaching career.

Utilizing this approach enables me to teach across the curriculum and to address my students' multifarious learning styles. In doing so, I make connections. For example, I use poetry to teach parts of speech. "Nounsense" poems, "Pronouns that are Personal" poems, and descriptive "Adjectives Abound" poetry illustrate a few kinds of students' poems included in an annual sixth-grade publication, *An Anthology of Poetry*. Thematic poetry is also reflected in our anthology.

Literature forms the foundation of my thematic teaching. During the course of our election unit, I read several books, including *D Is for Democracy* by Elissa Grodin and *So You Want to Be President* by Judith St. George and David Small. Following each read, students respond in writing in their free response journals.

This would be an opportunity for the children to reflect on something they heard or saw that was meaningful and to project their ideas and feelings about the subject. This information was valuable for further exploration in other assignments such as a compare/contrast essay about the candidates, a presidential debate, or a reader's theater performance.

For the 2005–2006 school year, I am beginning an A+ thematic unit on the Eastern Hemisphere with research papers. One class has been assigned ancient history, another class the Middle Ages, and the third sixth-grade class modern history. I have just collected these papers, and I have reports on everything from ancient Egypt, ancient Greece, and ancient China to the Renaissance, the Reformation, the French Revolution, World War II, the Holocaust, and the Iraq War.

We have many other activities planned for the balance of the school year. These reports will be presented to all the sixth graders along with accompanying visuals such as skits, models, posters, videos, and speakers, affording all the sixth graders, and ultimately the entire Cook School student body, the opportunity to learn about Eastern Hemisphere history and culture from ancient to modern times.

Again, literature will form the basis of my teaching as students will be comparing and contrasting types of governments and religions. They will be writing biographical poems about historical figures, and they will create a culminating PowerPoint presentation to be shared schoolwide.

Helpful Tips

- Borrow from the best. Be eclectic.
- Throughout my 30 years of teaching, I've seen many programs come and go. If a program has value, why dispose of it? For example, several years ago, the Accelerated Reader (AR) program was received as the answer to get all children to read. It worked. Library circulation in our school library increased from 12,000 checkouts per year to 34,000 checkouts per year, which continues to this date.
- I'll always remember a sixth-grade gifted and talented student. Six years ago, at the beginning of the school year, Richard came to me frustrated and said he hated to read. I told him he still had an AR goal to reach, whether he liked to read or not, as it was part of the language arts curriculum. Reluctantly at first, Richard read and made his goal each time. Later that year, in March, he came to me and said, "Mrs. Taylor, you taught me to love to read." Quickly I retorted, "You taught *yourself* to love to read by reading." Reading forms the foundation for writing. Although I see drawbacks in the AR program, such as being limited by books that have AR tests, the program, in my opinion, gets kids to read good children's literature. Now some new literacy programs seem to be

---

(Continued)

Helpful Tips (Continued)

> discouraging use of the AR program. Why not combine AR with other good new ideas such as "book talks"?
>
> ■ Cook sixth graders have an AR goal, but they also get points and grades for "book talks" on a book that is not AR but is one that they want to read. My tip is to be eclectic—combine the best ideas, the ones that work for you, from a variety of proven programs and sources.

CHAPTER 26

Using a Work of Art as a Stimulus for Writing

Diana W. McDougal

Cheyenne, Wyoming

A work of art can provide teachers of every discipline an excellent stimulus for building and improving both the writing and the critical thinking skills of adolescent students. By finding works of art that reflect the personal and career interests of your students, you can launch some powerful discussions, which will increase your students' understanding about context, content, process and procedure, problem solving, critical evaluation, and other rational and humanistic academic fundamentals.

In addition, current brain-based research is determining that learning is increased when the emotion chemicals of the brain are engaged. Because "artists create things that trigger emotions" (Zull, 2005), introducing actual images of artwork to your adolescent students can deeply engage them and therefore intensify learning in the classroom.

Art communicates visually beyond the restrictions of time, place, age, language, and culture, offering the opportunity to increase student understanding of the relevance of course-specific curriculum, as well as to increase student understanding of the connections among disciplines. The age-old adage "A picture is worth a thousand words" embodies the potential for increased understanding when using images or actual works of art to support learning in the classroom.

Conveniently, we live in an age of global visual communication; therefore, the resources for appropriate art images or actual works of art are nearly infinite. And using a work of art as a stimulus for writing fits any budget. Not only can course-appropriate images of art be found easily in traditional resources such as magazines and books, but they also can be found effortlessly on the Internet.

Actual works of art are as readily accessible as the nearest student pocket, purse or backpack, art classroom, market, or personal residence. Obviously, field trips to local, regional, national, and international galleries, museums, public parks, and historical centers offer works of art as stimuli and enrichment beyond the confines of the classroom and curriculum. A work of art is not only about the perceptions and beliefs of the artist, but it is also about the time, place, and culture from which it originates. What the viewer brings to the artwork is equally revealing. Therefore, a single work of art offers the opportunity to explore humanity on a variety of levels.

On a personal and individual level, artwork challenges each student to expose his or her own perceptions and beliefs. On a more global level, a work of art can open an avenue for exploring both common and unique human perceptions, historical and cultural influences, and the evolution or renaissance of beliefs and values. Writing exercises that require students to identify and explore the context, content, meaning, and purpose of a work of art build effective connections and tolerance for differences. Procedural parallels exist between the creative problem-solving process that involves the making of a work of art and those problem-solving processes of math, science, and technology. Therefore, writing exercises that require students to identify step-by-step, critical thinking processes and actual technical practices build multiple cognitive abilities.

It is not difficult to motivate students to write about works of art. Several strategies facilitate more immediate success for educators using art images and artwork as a stimulus for writing.

Reference

Zull, J. E. (2005). Arts, neuroscience and learning. *New Horizons for Learning.* (March). Retrieved November 15, 2006, from http://www.newhorizons.org/neuro/zull_2.htm.

Helpful Tips

- Select course-appropriate images that are not only of high interest to students but that will also help students discover the relevancies between course content and other disciplines and/or between personal interests and career choices.
- Select pieces that will evoke more questions than answers.
- Sequence writing exercises so that students begin with brief, quick responses. Plan subsequent exercises that begin to require more length and that move students from answers to questions.
- Model the process by beginning with one or two exemplars; then, as the writing exercises begin to build in expectations for more length and depth of thought, offer students choices both for the selection of artwork and also for the kind of writing response.

Selecting High-Interest Works of Art

- Obviously, there are regional differences that will affect student interest. Students in urban areas with easier access to actual and culturally significant works of art will be visually stimulated for writing by images much different than those students of rural areas, where the familiar artwork is most probably highly regional and economically influenced.

CHAPTER 27

Making a Move

James Darrell Harris

Lubbock, Texas

*A*fter I had been teaching happily in elementary for 5 years, there were suddenly fingernail prints in the pavement leading from my elementary campus to the junior high school down the street. Someone felt that a man was needed, for discipline purposes, in the Resource class, and I was "it." This was a move I didn't want to make. Like so many others, I had heard the horror stories of teaching junior high school. Now, 30 years later, I continue to enjoy the best teaching experience a person could have—teaching students with learning disabilities in junior high school.

Everyone tells me, "Kids this age don't like to write." However, one of the biggest obstacles to learning is the "note-writing" these early adolescents seem to immerse themselves in daily. After watching my students for a few days, I decided I would begin the task of learning to write without teaching the subject.

I began requiring my students to submit all requests to me in writing. This included going to the nurse, computer lab, office, library, restroom, and so on. Their requests had to state their reason for the request and three supporting sentences to expand upon the reason.

What I found was lots of students willing to write if they had a reason to do so. Over time, many of the students became excellent persuasive writers, and it wasn't too long until they were amenable to learning how to improve their skills.

In special education, there is never a shortage of challenges. I was soon confronted by the student who reverses letters and has tremendous problems with both reading and writing. I tried a number of techniques and became frustrated with my efforts. I wasn't to blame, however— this was a problem with the student's eyes, not my teaching. It didn't take too long before I stood before the truth: It *was* my problem! I'm the teacher. After much effort that went nowhere, it dawned on me that if the eyes were the problem, eliminate the use of the eyes. After all, nonsighted students learn to read and write.

I began my great adventure with a set of 3-inch plastic letters. The student I was working with was blindfolded during the lesson. I had him feel a letter, name it, make the sound of the letter, and write it. We took as much time as needed to master each letter. Finally, we began to do whole words and eventually complete sentences. I then took the blindfold off and retaught each lesson exactly as I had done when the student was blindfolded.

I understand that I wasn't being scientific, but the transfer of learning seemed to occur, and my student became a good reader and fell in love with writing. This is not a victory to be reported on a leading broadcast, but it made a difference to that student. I learned a good lesson. Being a teacher carries the responsibility of teaching, no matter how difficult the task or how impossible the problem.

Yes, I teach writing successfully with many of the standard methods, but when a student presents a special challenge, I have to be creative and use what works. If I accomplish little else, I would like to put to rest the notion that children of junior high age don't like to write. In point of fact, they love to write. The challenge for the teacher is finding a way to make writing relevant. One of my teaching experiences allowed me the opportunity to teach children who were in the hospital for a prolonged time. A particular 11-year-old taught me a lesson that will be imprinted in my mind forever. He was a terminal cancer patient.

Each day that I arrived in his hospital room to teach him was a day of absolute joy for me. His bright smile against his ebony skin lit the room with joy. I often wondered to myself how a youngster who knew he would soon die could be so happy. I couldn't teach him enough. He was so eager and tried so hard. One day I asked him, "Why do you want to learn to write so badly?" His reply was simple and honest. "When I get to heaven, God will want his angels to read him stories and write him poems." I understood that every child has a reason to learn and that each wants to learn. My job is really the easy part. I only have to find a way to teach them.

Index

**CORWIN
PRESS**

The Corwin Press logo—a raven striding across an open book—represents the union of courage and learning. Corwin Press is committed to improving education for all learners by publishing books and other professional development resources for those serving the field of PreK–12 education. By providing practical, hands-on materials, Corwin Press continues to carry out the promise of its motto: **"Helping Educators Do Their Work Better."**

Franklin Pierce College Library

00166327